THE HISTORIC EPISCOPATE

THE
HISTORIC
EPISCOPATE

IN THE FULLNESS
OF THE CHURCH

Seven essays by
Priests of the Church of England

Edited by
KENNETH M. CAREY
Principal of Westcott House, Cambridge

dacre press
westminster

FIRST PUBLISHED 1954
DACRE PRESS: A. AND C. BLACK LTD
4, 5 AND 6 SOHO SQUARE, LONDON, W.1

MADE IN GREAT BRITAIN
PRINTED BY THE BOWERING PRESS, PLYMOUTH

INTRODUCTION

THE idea of this book came to a group of friends in the summer of 1951. We were all old members of Westcott House and though there were, and are, considerable differences of theological outlook between us we were united in feeling a deep perplexity about the discussions which had followed the 1950 debates in the Convocations of Canterbury and York on the subject of the Church of South India. It was not that we could see any easy solution to that problem, such as abandoning the historic position of the Church of England about episcopacy, and were disappointed that many did not share our views. We are all in fact High Churchmen in the sense that we all hold a high doctrine of the Church and believe in the exercise of the apostolic ministry of the whole Church through the historic episcopate.

We were perplexed rather because it seemed to us that a great deal of the discussion in the Church was being carried on in considerable ignorance of the real issues involved and along lines which previous debates had shown to be blind alleys. There was on the one hand a great deal of wild and loose talk about the new Church in India;[1] and on the other hand it seemed that many people were trying to debate the subject in ways which were irrelevant.

Furthermore our perplexity seemed to be widely shared; at that time about half our group was working in parishes and there seemed no doubt that great numbers of clergy and laity were aware of a challenge coming from the new Church and yet deeply apprehensive that the challenge could only be met by sacrificing some point of principle. The Church of England indeed seemed, in this matter, to be rather like an old lady who gets flustered in the middle of a crowded

---

[1] e.g., I remember one very high dignatory remarking that the comparatively conciliatory tone of the 1950 Convocations did not really matter because in five years' time the Church of South India would have become so Protestant that no one in it would want union with the Church of England! Other examples of this sort of comment could be quoted.

5

street. She hears a confusion of voices; she sees a number of different ways; she begins to doubt why she has come and still more where she is meant to go. In the end to the great danger of herself and others she is tempted to stay where she is.

It is of course true that the Church of England does stand in the middle of the ecumenical road. She hears the voices of Rome and Istanbul, Geneva and the Central Hall. She sees one way labelled 'Intercommunion', another labelled 'Apostolic Succession', a third labelled 'Statesmanship'. She is very tempted to try the third, though in her heart she believes that it does not lead anywhere. To make matters worse, she has begun to distrust her own guides; time was when she would have followed any strong lead by the Bishops, but the Bishops speak with an uncertain voice: till recently, too, she had an awe and reverence for anything that was said by the scholars, but in these last twenty years she has heard scholars shouting themselves hoarse on either side of her. She has in fact begun to doubt both episcopal and academic authority. She stands where she did in the middle of the road and she does not lack guides to tell her that that is where she ought to remain.

But that is what she cannot do. The time for delay is rapidly passing. The stream of traffic is increasing from every direction; and there is no island of safety in the middle. The Church of England must make a decision. She cannot stay where she is.

So far in our discussions we were agreed, and we recognized that over the question of South India the Church of England was already committed to making a decision. The Convocations of 1950 had in effect postponed a judgment for five years. It seemed to us, therefore, that it would be worth while to re-examine the evidence and to try to find some new approach to the problem. We agreed that the old *esse* v. *bene esse* debate was sterile; we believed that too much time had already been spent on the vain attempt to find in the New Testament conclusive evidence for any one type of ministry; and we were bound by our convictions to reject a solution which sacrificed any real point of principle. Above all we recognized that any new approach must be both theological and historical. So we planned a rough draft of the book and went away to think about the particular section which each of us had agreed to write. To us the most remarkable and encouraging fact about the whole endeavour was the discovery when we met again after several months that we had all arrived at more or less the same conclusion. And we believe that we have seen a solution which is true in theology and fair to history and which in no way compromises the beliefs of our own church.

This book is however no plea for hasty and ill-considered action in the wide sphere of ecumenicity. It is true that what the Church of England decides about the Church of South India will *eventually* determine to a large degree her attitude towards the Nonconformists in this country. We must however be quite clear about this. Full Communion with the Church of South India involves us in agreement with a Church which has already accepted the historic episcopate; doubtless there are subsidiary questions about which many Anglicans will require further elucidation before they can happily commit themselves, but the basic conditions of the Lambeth Quadrilateral are, in the express intention of that Church, in process of being fulfilled. Intercommunion, still more full organic union, with Nonconformists in this country is a different problem. An Anglican may well believe with Bishop Lightfoot that we have no right to un-church a body of Christians simply because they have not got the historic episcopate; he may accept the fact that in matters of faith there is no outstanding difference between the Nonconformists and ourselves; he may even be convinced that a far greater measure of occasional Intercommunion would bring the goal of full unity nearer; but he may still believe that full communion with them at the moment would retard rather than accelerate the Unity of the Church. In our relations with the Nonconformists in this country there are still many problems to be resolved before effective steps can be taken towards unity. There is the problem of discipline; there is the problem of what has been called 'non-theological factors'; above all, there is the problem of sheer indifference on the part of the rank and file of both sides. Perhaps the plainest way of putting it is that we will never get reunion with the Nonconformists in this country until both sides really want it, and until we can show the Nonconformists a *theological* interpretation of episcopacy which does not involve a denial of their own past.

With the Church of South India the case is far different. With her the danger is that among the great and difficult questions—Communism, finance, industrial evangelism and a hundred others—with which the Church of England is beset, the very existence of a Church many thousand miles away may be shelved and disregarded. Yet we cannot allow ourselves to forget what has happened since the inauguration of the new Church. Both on theological and pastoral grounds the Church of South India is in a quite different position from the Nonconformists in this country. She has accepted the historic episcopate and she has great need of the help which full union with the Church of England would bring her.

It has been said again and again that the question of Reunion is not a matter of pastoral expediency but of theological truth. We recognize that the Church of England must not take precipitate action about Reunion simply because of the menace of Communism in India or because of the difficulties of evangelism for a Church which is deprived of the help of one of her parent bodies. Nevertheless, if it is GOD's will that the wounds in the Body of Christ should be healed it would not be suprising that we should find ourselves after Union better equipped to offer to the world a true alternative to Communism and to bring to the pagan multitudes a more compelling Gospel. In the sight of GOD there can be no divorce between what is theologically true and what is pastorally necessary. And if it is the will of GOD that the Churches should be reunited not in some remote and unimaginable future but now, as soon as the sin and wilfulness of men can be overcome, then it is surely the duty of every Christian to think out seriously and deeply what steps can be taken without delay towards Reunion.

INTRODUCTION

It is because we believe that there is a way by which the Church of England can retain all the truth which she has inherited from the past and at the same time advance towards Reunion that we have written this book. For the most part we have limited ourselves to a discussion of what seems to us to be the most vital aspects for Anglicans of the problem of the relation of the Church to its Ministry. In pursuing this aim we have first tried to set the whole question in its biblical perspective (Chapters I and II); we have then gone on to consider those periods of Church history which have been vital in the formation of Anglican theology (Chapters III, IV and V); the penultimate chapter advances a view of the theology of episcopacy which we believe to be both true and Anglican and therefore preferable to either of the two alternatives commonly advanced from the two wings of the Church of England. This view is of course implicit in the earlier essays.

Theology, however, must be relevant to life. The final chapter discusses the application of these principles here and now to the urgent problem of our relations with the Church of South India. No doubt when the Convocations meet in 1955 there will be much searching of hearts and any agreed decision will need all the wisdom and skill of which the Church of England is capable. What is more, any decision which will command general agreement is bound to involve some of its members in a change of mind. It is because we believe that such a change is possible (indeed, we have found it among ourselves) without sacrificing principle or compromising loyalty that we offer this book to the Church as a contribution to the fresh thought which must precede the decision in 1955.

KENNETH M. CAREY

WESTCOTT HOUSE
CAMBRIDGE.
February 1954

CONTENTS

KINGDOM, CHURCH AND MINISTRY

J. A. T. Robinson

THE contemporary issues facing the Church, as she gropes to regain her shattered unity, in South India as elsewhere, can be clarified and resolved only if we take the trouble to understand her order and her orders as history has fashioned them and history interpreted them. That is why this book carries the title, perhaps inevitably, of *The Historic Episcopate*. But the aim of this chapter is to see this whole undertaking in theological perspective, set, that is to say, in the total biblical picture of what God in Christ has done, is doing, and will do to His world. For it would be false to assume that a particular interpretation of the episcopate, or any judgment of Church order in isolation, could of itself decide the issue of our relations with the Church of South India.

It has been a noticeable feature of many of the judgments made upon South India that they have sprung from certain *a priori* 'truths' or 'principles' to which geographical distance and the contemporary historical context are strictly irrelevant. They have not been made out of the situation of the South Indian Church, let alone out of the situation of South Indian politics, but have been laid down from this country on the basis of certain preconceived absolutes of Catholic order. Even the Lambeth Report of 1948 reads somewhat like a committee of examiners sitting with a key before them marking the various essays in reunion submitted by a bunch of candidates from Ceylon, North India, Persia, Nigeria, America, etc. The result of this procedure has been to produce judgments on South India which are apt to appear unrealistic, if not positively exasperating, to those on the spot, and, by their isolation of Church order, strangely remote from the promptings either of evangelistic urgency or of political realism. Those Christians, in turn, whose judgments are influenced by such pressures are accused of bartering Catholic truth for short-term expediency; and the familiar sterile debate ensues.

The purpose of this essay is to suggest that we are in this impasse for theological and not merely for ecclesiastical reasons. The deadlock is with us fundamentally because the priorities, and therefore the proportion, of biblical truth have been upset. Without going back further, we may see how this happened in the debate on Church unity as it was staged in the period 1920–1939. Of the two main parties to it, the Anglo-Catholics started from a high doctrine of the Ministry, as defined and guaranteed in the Apostolic Succession. By this every proposal was tested, for on it all else was made to hang. The doctrine of the Church was directly dependent upon it (no Bishop, no Church); and any doctrine of the Kingdom, that is, of God's universal rule in history, was subordinated to His design for the Church, and could in this matter be disregarded. The influence of what God might be doing in the contemporary world (e.g. through secular forces making for world unity, economic collectivism or national self-consciousness) was at best irrelevant and at worst dangerous to the principles of Catholic order. On the other side, the Liberals started from a doctrine of the Kingdom—though, with the emphasis heavily on the *Kingdom* rather than on the Kingdom of *God*, it is difficult to call it a high one. At any rate, their doctrine of the Church was lower. The Church was the most obvious agency, though by no means the exclusive one, for building the Kingdom of God on earth; in practice it was subordinated either to the social gospel or to the religious experience of the individual. Meanwhile, their doctrine of the ministry was lower still—a matter largely of organization—and the stickling of their opponents over orders and succession seemed to them to betray a well-nigh mediaeval irrelevance to the Will of God for their generation.

In this debate, aided partly by strength of principle and partly by the direction of world events, the Anglo-Catholics in large measure prevailed, to the increasing disillusionment of the Liberals. It was not that in any decisive sense they won the prize—the Liberals had at least impressed their consoling conviction that in this game all might win and have prizes—but that they did succeed in fixing the terms of the motion. In consequence, when the issue became crystallized in the discussions of the forties, the question of South India was debated by Catholic and Evangelical alike almost entirely on the Anglo-Catholic priority. The Church must be judged by the Ministry, and the Kingdom by the Church. It was equally clear to those who knew South India itself, either before or after Union (again whether they were by tradition Catholic or Evangelical), that this priority made much of the debate extraordinarily unreal.[1]

In this rather depressing situation the most significant new factor has been the revival in biblical theology, of which in this field the Bishop of Durham's *The Gospel and the Catholic Church* was the harbinger. The result of this revival has been to confirm the position of neither party. Its most immediate and obvious consequence was to confound the Liberals. It convicted them of having pitched their doctrine alike of the Kingdom, the Church and the Ministry too low. The work of Sir Edwyn Hoskyns and his school was welcomed as grist to the Anglo-Catholic mill. But of greater significance in the long run will perhaps be the question which this biblical theology has put against the whole Anglo-Catholic sequence of priorities.

The renewed interest in the theology of the New Testament has revealed indeed that nothing less than the highest doctrine of the ministry is compatible with the teaching and practice of Apostolic Christianity. For the Christian ministry is no other than the ministry, the liturgy, of Christ Himself as He channels through preaching and sacrament, through forgiveness and healing, the continuous creation of the New World wrought on Easter Day. God, wrote St. Paul, 'has empowered us as ministers of the New Order' (2 Cor. iii. 6) and has 'vested in us' the ministry of the reconciliation

---

[1] An illustration of this is the way in which the decision of the Society for the Propagation of the Gospel at home not to support any ministers of the Church of South India failed to carry with it more than a small minority of its missionaries on the spot.

achieved in Christ (2 Cor. v. 18 f). 'We are therefore Christ's official representatives' (*presbeuomen*) (2 Cor. v. 20)—with the corollary, as Jesus said, that 'he that rejecteth you, rejecteth me' (Luke x. 16). There could be no higher doctrine of the Christian ministry.

But the Ministry is the ministry of Christ only as it is the ministry of the Church.[1] All that is said of the ministry in the New Testament is said not of individuals nor of some apostolic college or 'essential ministry' but of the whole Body, whatever the differentiation of function within it. This follows because the whole life of Christ is given to the Church to be possessed *in solidum*: the Spirit, the New Life, the Priesthood, everything, belongs to each only as it belongs to all. In Pauline language this is expressed by saying that Christ's life is now lived and given 'Bodywise' (*somatikos*), not individually but corporately, so that the fullness of God now resides in Him as it resides at the same time in us His members (Col. ii. 9 f).[2] Consequently, every ministry in the Church, as it exists on behalf of Christ (2 Cor. v. 20, *hyper Christou*), automatically exists for the sake of the Body (Eph. iv. 11 f; cf. Col. i. 24, *hyper tou somatos*). Its authority and validity[3] derive from

[1] Not, of course, of the Church apart from Christ, any more than of Christ apart from the Church, but of Christ in the Church. Hence the tension felt by writers in *The Apostolic Ministry* (26 f; 171–81; 511–15) between the ministry of the Church and the ministry (of the apostles) to the Church is an unreal one. There are not 'two conceptions of the relation of the ministry to the Church' respectively in 1 Cor. 12 and Eph. 4. In both the various ministries (including that of the apostolate) are set by Christ *in* the Body and *for* the Body. *Cf.* L. Newbigin, *The Reunion of the Church*, 167: 'The ministerial commission is from the living Christ in and over the Church which is His Body'.

[2] For the exegesis of this and similar passages, cf. my book, *The Body*, 68–71.

[3] I use the word 'validity' (from the Latin *validus*, strong) of the authorization which a ministry and its sacraments has from the Church. This may clearly admit of degrees and is open to human judgment.

It should be distinguished from 'efficacy' which is the assertion that Christ uses the orders or sacraments in question for His redeeming work of grace. This efficacy may indeed be impaired by sin and disunity, but it is a matter, thankfully, which no man can judge (except, partially, by its fruits). We may rest in the assurance that 'the unworthiness of the minister hinders not the effect of the sacrament'. (Article XXVI.)

The word 'defective' is best reserved to denote absence of 'intention' to do what the Church does. This again can admit of degree, but is in the nature of the case more difficult to determine.

In retaining the term 'validity' as here defined, I wish to express my concurrence with later writers in this book who reject it in the sense of what is 'guaranteed' or 'legitimate'.

Christ-in-His-Body. The only valid ministry is that of the *Totus Christus*. Every ministry is invalidated, weakened in its authority, to the degree that behind it lies the authorization only of a broken part of the Body and not the 'It seemed good to the Holy Ghost and to us' of the whole Catholic Church.[1] To establish the validity of the ministry on grounds independent of the authority of the living Church (e.g. by linear succession of episcopal consecration), and then to judge whether a church is part of the Body by whether it has a valid ministry, is to invert the whole New Testament conception. It is to subordinate the doctrine of the Church to the doctrine of the Ministry; whereas the New Testament bids us have as high a doctrine in the Ministry as we like, providing always our doctrine of the Church is higher.

But it does not stop there. For as the Ministry is a function of the Church, so the Church is a function of the Kingdom, of the universal Lordship of God in Christ.

The Kingdom of God, rather even than the People of God, is the controlling category of biblical theology for both Old and New Testaments. The message of the New Testament is that this Kingship has been realized in history once and for all in the victory which God 'wrought in Christ, when he raised him from the dead, and made him to sit at his right hand in the heavenly places, far above all rule, and authority, and power, and dominion, and every name that is named, not only in this world, but also in that which is to come: and he put all things in subjection under his feet' (Eph. i. 20–2). But this statement leads immediately to the assertion that God 'gave him to be head over all things to the Church, which is his body, the fulness of him who all in all is being filled' (i. 22 f.). What, then, is the relation of the Church to the *fait accompli* of the universal kingship of God in Christ?

St. Paul gives his answer later, in Eph. iii. 10 f. In Christ, as he has said elsewhere (Col. i. 20), the whole constitution of the universe has now been transformed: through the Cross all things in heaven and earth have been reconciled and reduced. Within this total event, the purpose of the Church is,

[1] Cf. O. C. Quick, *The Christian Sacraments*, 143–7; *The Doctrines of the Creed*, 340f.

B   15

by proclaiming to the whole universe the truth of what has been done to it, to translate this victory into open acknowledgment and moral obedience. It serves as the instrument of the Kingdom, 'to the intent that now unto the principalities and the powers in the heavenly places might be made known *through the Church* the manifold wisdom of God, according to the eternal purpose which he purposed in Christ Jesus our Lord'.

The Church stands between the Kingdom accomplished and the Kingdom acknowledged. Its task is tied to the proclamation of that Kingdom and its time to the consummation of the age in the manifest vindication of God in Christ (Matt. xxviii. 19 f.). Until that moment, it forms the covenant people of the New Order, the first-fruits of God's renewed creation (James i. 18), in which 'the open consecration of a part marks the destiny of the whole' (Westcott). Itself the resurrection Body of Christ, humanity as it has so far acknowledged its redemption, it is set within the present body of history to work that transformation whereby eventually the whole shall be conformed to its goal, the Body of His glory (Phil. iii. 21). 'For as in Adam all die, so also in Christ shall all be made alive'. 'But', St. Paul continues, 'each in his own order: Christ the first-fruits; then they that are Christ's (i.e. the Church), at his coming. Then cometh the end, when he shall deliver up the kingdom to God, even the Father, when he shall have abolished all rule and all authority and power' (1 Cor. xv. 22–4).

Nothing could be more exalted than the doctrine of the Church which the New Testament presents—indeed it is impossible to be a biblical theologian without being a high Churchman. The Church is the carrier now of the Divine glory (*endoxon*, Eph. v, 27), the pledge and the instrument of all creation's destiny. Yet ultimately the New Testament subjects the Church to the Kingdom.

This means that the Church stands always under the judgment of the Kingdom. It means that Christians and all Christian policies are to be assessed not simply by their relation to the Church but by their relation to the Kingdom. Not all those who have lived in Christ's 'name' (Matt. vii.

21–3), nor all those who have been incorporated into Him through the sacraments (1 Cor. x. 1–12), will for that reason enter the Kingdom of God. The Church lives ever with the parable of the sheep and the goats, with its reminder that from the foundation of the world the Father's kingdom has been prepared for many who have not 'known'. Its final condemnation is still that like the Church of Jewry it should shut up the Kingdom of heaven against men (Matt. xxiii. 13).

Just as the New Testament bids us have as high a doctrine of the ministry as we like, as long as our doctrine of the Church is higher, so it commands us have as high a doctrine of the Church as we may, provided our doctrine of the Kingdom is higher. And this conclusion is of no mere academic consequence. It must govern all our assessments as Christians, including those about Church union. It should, for instance, make us chary of any form of argument (whether negative or positive) which suggests that if the Church of South India possess a certain ministry, then it is a valid Church, and if it is a valid Church, then it is God's will for South India and the world. It should make us equally hesitant of dismissing as mere expediency arguments of evangelism or even of politics. In the Last Day it is conceivable that the capturing of the new Asia for Christ may be that to which episcopal pedigree is a matter of expediency rather than the other way round. But if we are to be true to the New Testament, it would be better not to use the category of expediency at all. For nothing can be 'mere' expediency to those whose whole function is defined as 'speeding (*speudontes*) the coming of the day of God' (2 Pet. iii, 12).

It is no accident that the failure to relate the Church properly to the Kingdom should issue also in the failure to relate the Ministry properly to the Church. Both reflect a more fundamental failure to retain the eschatological perspective of the New Testament, to which reference has just been made. We shall not get our theology of the Church and the Ministry right until we get our eschatology right. This may seem a remote and windy statement, but it is the contention of this opening chapter that much of our trouble has come precisely from poring over too small an

17

area of the map. We need to consult our co-ordinates again.

To hold the Church constantly under the Kingdom is to relate it dynamically to the two great moments of Christ's sovereignty over the world—the finished work of Calvary and His final coming in glory to claim His new creation. The ministry of the Church is the present ministry 'between the times' of the Christ who has come and will come. This ministry derives its character and its power from these two mighty acts. It is a making present, a bringing into effective operation in the here and now, of all that happened in Palestine, all that will happen at the Parousia. This is the inner meaning of everything that the Church does—in preaching and baptism and eucharist, in forgiveness, healing and discipline.

The New Testament doctrine of episcopacy illustrates very well this essential polarity which characterizes the whole Christian ministry. The *episcope* of the Church (that is, of Christ in His Church) is that which stands between, and mediates to this present age, the *episcope*, the visitation, of God to His people in Christ's first coming and in His last. 'The day of visitation' stood in the Old Testament for the Day of the Lord, when God would reign among the peoples as King and Judge (Isa. x. 3; cf. Hos. ix. 7; Jer. v. 29). The proclamation of the Gospel was that in Jesus God had thus 'visited His people' (Luke i. 68; vii. 16). Rejected by Jerusalem, who 'knew not the time of her visitation' (Luke xix. 44), God had further, so the primitive Church was to be shewn, 'visited the Gentiles, to take out of them a people for his name' (Acts xv. 14). But even in this fulfilment the great 'day of visitation' was not yet exhausted. It waited still to be consummated in the final advent of Christ (1 Pet. ii. 12). Between these two moments (and re-calling and anticipating them in present action) the *episcope* is committed to the Church in its ministry to 'exercise the oversight' (1 Pet. v. 2), till 'the chief Shepherd shall be manifested' (1 Pet. v. 4), the Shepherd who is Himself the *Episcopos* of souls (1 Pet. ii. 25).

The episcopacy, like the whole ministry and indeed existence of the Church, is 'validated' by the mighty acts of the Kingdom. The final guarantee that these events are themselves valid, grounded, that is, in the authority of God and stronger therefore than anything else, is an eschatological one—the assurance that in the end it will still be 'this same Jesus' crowned Lord of history and not another. It is thus in terms of eschatology that the Church and its ministry receive their ultimate validation (cf. Matt. xvi. 18 f.; Luke xii, 32; xxii, 29 f.).

But very soon in the course of Christian history the subordination of all to the vindication of the Parousia, and with it the subjection of the Church to the surety and judgment of the Kingdom, slipped away. The Church became her own guarantor, even if not yet identified theologically with the Kingdom. And this had profound repercussions. For without the guarantee of the End everything was made to rest on continuity with the Beginning. The Church as the eschatological community of the Messiah gave place to the Church as the extension of the Incarnation. Hence the concern, from the subapostolic age onwards, with preserving the form of sound doctrine once delivered to the saints, with pseudonymous writings to perpetuate the cover of apostolic aegis, and above all with insuring continuity through episcopal succession. The ministry becomes grounded, not, as in the New Testament, in the present gift of the Church's ascended Head (Eph. iv, 8–12), but in the Jesus of history. It is validated by 'looking *back* to Christ as its source, not by way of "the Church" but by way of the apostolic line of descent', a descent derived from 'the Lord Himself *in the days of His flesh*' (K. Kirk in *The Apostolic Ministry*, pp. 49, 52. Italics mine). Adrift from its anchor of hope, the Church grasped the life-line of historical succession. Shorn of its guarantee in the Kingdom, it sought its title-deeds in the Ministry. The episcopate, instead of being an organ of its life, became the hall-mark of its very existence, 'the authentic guarantee of its claim to be the Body of Christ among men' (ibid., p. 46): *ubi episcopus, ibi ecclesia.*[1]

[1] An interesting parallel is provided in the history of the Old Israel by the reversal after the Exile of the relative position of the law and the covenant. 'Whereas they [the laws] were formerly subordinate to the covenant, they now become *conditions* for belonging to the covenant. . . . Not the community, the covenant, is the presupposition of the Law, but the Law is the presupposition for the community.' (A. Bentzen, *Introduction to the Old Testament*, I, 231.)

It should be added that the last emphasis on the *episcopate* rather than the whole institutional continuity of the Church itself, as the locus of the guarantee, is a modern, if not a peculiarly Anglican, development (though it was made possible by Augustine's unfortunate detachment of validity of orders from the authority of the Church). What was for Ignatius a matter of order and ecclesiastical discipline ('Wheresoever the Bishop shall appear, there let the people be'; *ad Smyrn.*, 8) has become for the modern Anglo-Catholic a matter of faith, that without a Bishop there is no Church. Bishop Newbigin points out very clearly how the Anglican who desires to use this argument is forced to isolate the Bishop from the Church, and to prove 'that the authority of bishops to ordain and consecrate is by itself, and apart from the unity and continuity of the whole Body, the authority upon which the existence of the Church depends' (op. cit., p. 83).[1] 'It is only upon the basis of this claim that it is possible at the same time to assert the duty of excommunicating non-episcopal Churches and to deny the right of Rome to excommunicate episcopal. Anglican writers who undertake the discharge of this exacting war upon two fronts have to prove that the plenitude of Christ's authority rests in such an exclusive manner in the hands of the historically continuous episcopate that where—on the one hand—a part of the episcopate separates itself from the rest of Christendom, there the Church still exists, but that where—on the other hand— a Church acts without the authority of the episcopate, it places itself in a position where it must be excommunicated. The plenitude of Christ's commission therefore rests in the bishops, and is retained by them even when they separate themselves from the rest of the Church' (ibid. pp. 151-2).

Bishop Newbigin cites the judgment of Cardinal Newman quoted by Dr. Kirk, that 'Catholics believe that their orders are valid because they belong to the true Church; Anglicans believe they belong to the true Church because their orders are valid'. He points out that the former proposition applies even more strongly to Orthodoxy[1] than to mediaeval and

[1] Cf. O. C. Quick, *The Christian Sacraments*, 137 f.
[1] Cf. S. Bulgakov's statement in *The Ministry and the Sacraments*, 102 f., quoted by Newbigin, *op. cit.*, 165

modern Romanism. Indeed, the Anglo-Catholic position of the last hundred years is a historical curiosity. 'The tragedy', he says, 'of the position . . . is that in the attempt to justify itself against Rome and the East it is compelled to excommunicate the rest, yet by this dual warfare it can gain the acceptance of neither. What might have been a steppingstone for mutual traffic between separated bodies is turned into a fortified and isolated island inaccessible to either side' (ibid., p. 189).

What conclusions should then be drawn from this argument? That continuity is a thing of no value, that the historic episcopate and apostolic succession are matters indifferent to the Body of Christ and the Gospel of the Kingdom? By no means. A Church without continuity in time is as sinful and broken as a Church without unity in space. Every movement towards Christian reunion must take both into account as of equal importance. And there can be no retreat into the invisible Church. *Organic*, and not merely spiritual or doctrinal, continuity is as necessary to the fullness of the Church as *organic* unity. And each of these finds its focus in the historic episcopate, the outward and visible expression at once of the Church's catholicity and of its apostolicity. For in the episcopate[1] is embodied alike the dependence of every congregation upon the one Church of God, of which it is but the local manifestation, and the continuity of the whole in doctrine, liturgy and authority with the historic events in which it is founded.[2] Every scheme for Christian unity must come to terms with the historic episcopate; for *despite* it the Church cannot in fact be fully one, catholic or apostolic. If

[1] 'Episcopacy' is here being used theologically as the office of oversight within the Body, the seat of authority and the fount of ministry, rather than as a particular form of ecclesiastical organization. That the *episcope* of the Church should have settled in the shape of monepiscopacy (rather than been vested in presbyteral episcopacy) cannot in itself be regarded as inevitable nor necessitated by the institution of Jesus, the form of the Gospel, or the *monarchia* of the Godhead. That the *episcope* has taken this pattern is simply one of the facts given (by God and history) to be taken into account in the discussion of Church unity. That 'the coming great Church' could be other than monepiscopal (with whatever modifications) is not a historical possibility. But the important thing is not that the Protestant Churches should 'take bishops into their system' (some already have them), but that the *episcope* of the Church should be unified, in time as in space, round what is, historically, the only given focus.

[2] Cf. A. M. Ramsey, *The Gospel and the Catholic Church*, ch. VI.

we did not believe this, we should not be writing this book.

But what we are concerned to deny (as unbiblical, unhistorical and unanglican) is a particular interpretation of the episcopate which would automatically unchurch any part of the Body that for historical reasons has failed to preserve it. For that is to exalt it as a precondition of the Church, whereas the only precondition of the Church is the Kingdom of God. We affirm that the episcopate is dependent on the Church, and not the Church on the episcopate. We believe its possession to be a necessary mark of the Church's fullness, rather than an indispensable qualification for being a part. It is not what makes the Church the Church—so that in exclusion from it everything falls to the ground. But in repudiation of it the Church can never express the plenitude of its Being as the one Body of Christ in history.

The specific application of this to the situation in South India is not the function of this chapter. Before that is possible, it is necessary to see how the Church has worked it out in other crises of her life. But our immediate concern here has been to show that the fundamental conception of the episcopate for which we are contending is not in itself a matter of history but of theology. Moreover, the inversion of the relation between Church and Ministry which underlies the interpretation we dispute is not simply an historical accident. It derives from a deeper theological failure properly to relate the Church to the total rule of God over His world and in particular to eschatology. Until the issue of episcopacy is faced, like every other theological issue, at that level and in that context, the reiteration of historical arguments and confessional statements will not see us very much further.

THE MINISTRY IN THE NEW TESTAMENT

W. H. Vanstone

To consider the question whether, on the basis of the New
Testament evidence, episcopacy is essential to the Church, is
to be aware at once of a certain incongruity. The very
framing of the question implies a degree of reflection on the
nature of the Church—on its essential and non-essential
characteristics—which could not possibly be expected at so
early a date; it implies a crystallization of technical terms too
advanced for a society which was still evolving its distinctive
concepts and language; and it implies a discursive, analytical
approach to theological problems which is far removed from
the immediacy of New Testament experience. We have only
to translate the question into Greek to realize how strangely
it would sound in any New Testament context.

It does not follow from this that the New Testament
'knows nothing' of episcopacy in the technical sense implied
by the question; if the word 'episcopacy' is unfamiliar in the
New Testament, so also is the word 'Christianity', and it
would be quixotic in the extreme to say that the New Testament 'knows nothing of Christianity'. But it does follow that
a decisive answer to the question posed is not to be expected.
The question must be, so to speak, translated before the New
Testament evidence can be brought to bear upon it; and
what is to be the norm of a correct or adequate translation?
We are perplexed not so much by the paucity and ambiguity
of the New Testament evidence itself as by our own un-
certainty about the *kind* of evidence which we require; do we
require, for instance, proof of the existence of a certain
institution in New Testament times, or, on the other hand,
proof of the recognition of a certain principle? To put the
same dilemma in another form: would it be possible to com-

pose, in something akin to New Testament Greek, a number of texts which, by common consent, would be decisive for the present problem, and, if so, what would the content of these texts be?

It must be admitted that one particular short cut to the solution of the problem is, at first sight, attractive. 'Either,' it might be said, 'there was an episcopate in the New Testament Church, or there was not. If there was, then, whether or not it was essential in theory, it is there for our imitation in practice. If there was not, then clearly an "essential" episcopate is out of the question. Let us stick to the evidence on this particular point of fact.' And so we might be led, on the one hand, to reiterate Lightfoot's magisterial verdict on the identity of Presbyteri and Episcopi in the relevant New Testament passages; and so, by equating the episcopate with the lesser ministry, to deny it any unique significance; or, on the other hand, we might point to those shadowy figures— 'them which have the rule over you' in Hebrews XIII, 'them which . . . are over you in the Lord' in 1 Thess. v. 12, and 'such persons as Stephanas', to whom the Corinthian Christians owe both honour and obedience—claiming that here at least is the embryonic form of a distinctive, supra-presbyterial order. Even if, at the present, the weight of evidence is not conclusive on either side, it might be argued that further research along these lines is the short and straight path to the solution of our problem. But the objection is, of course, that this path is altogether too short and too straight.

In fact we might be warned of the practical difficulty of such a procedure by the results of the attempt in the 'Apostolic Ministry' to pursue it further. It is generally agreed that the well-known passage, Titus i. 5–7 points to the identification in the writer's mind of the terms *presbyteros* and *episcopos*: 'that thou shouldest set in order the things that are wanting and ordain *presbyterous* in every city, as I appointed thee: if anyone be blameless, the husband of one wife, having believing children who are not charged with riotousness or unruly; for an *episcopos* must be blameless . . .' In order to refute the traditional interpretation of this passage,

Dr. Farrer in the 'Apostolic Ministry' (p. 159 ff.) is reduced to these expedients: he places a heavy stop after 'as I appointed thee', and attaches the subsequent conditional clause (v. 5) to verse 6. Four times, he remarks, the phrase 'if any . . .' occurs elsewhere in the Pastoral Epistles; in each case it is to be construed with what follows, not with what precedes: so also here. 'If anyone be blameless . . . (here's your man); for the bishop must be blameless . . .' But the insuperable difficulty to this is the tacit introduction of a main clause 'here's your man', of which there is no trace or semblance in the Greek. The comparisons which are made with the four other passages in the Pastorals are irrelevant; in each of them 'if any' is followed by a main clause in a perfectly normal way. This is not the case in Titus i. 6. 'If any' here must refer back to the preceding clause. The sentence must mean 'Appoint as presbyters anyone who . . .'. Further, Dr. Farrer supposes that the writer, having instructed Titus to appoint presbyters, goes on immediately to give the qualifications for the quite distinct office of Bishop—about the appointment to which no word has yet been said. The writer says nothing about the qualifications of presbyters, whose appointment he has just mentioned, but something about the qualifications of the Bishop, of whose appointment he has said nothing. This interpretation of the thought of the passage is as tortuous as that of the syntax.

The resort of a distinguished scholar to such expedients must warn us that a limit has been reached in the interpretation of those New Testament books which bear directly on the question before us. We can be reasonably certain that the term *episcopos* did not denote, for the New Testament writers, an office distinct from and superior to the presbyterate; on the other hand there are some hints that, in certain churches, under no precise or commonly recognized title such an office was known. Further than this it is not possible to go. And we must ask again what precisely would be gained by the discovery of further evidence on this particular point. If the aim is simply the exact repetition of New Testament order in its outward form, then, whether or not we are committed to an episcopate in the contemporary church, we are certainly committed to contemporary orders of apostles and prophets and to other eccentricities which would be acceptable only to a naive biblicism or a pedantic antiquarianism. If on the other hand—and surely the truth lies here—the aim is the preservation or the recovery of the true enduring life of the church, then the question will not be of the number of offices, of their titles and of their relation to one another, but of the meaning and power of church order as such. We need not know the precise form of ecclesiastical order at a particular epoch, but the meaning of order as such in the life of the church. Purely factual research must be married to reflection and historical understanding before it can become normative for theology.

From this point of view there is a greater possibility of progress in the approach to episcopacy not in terms of a concrete institution, but in terms of authority. If church order is a matter not of titles and precedence but of the manner in which the church lives, then the power and weight and decisiveness of the authority exercised by a few men in the early church cannot be excluded from this discussion. What ever may have been the recognized institutions within the churches of Thessalonica and Corinth, it is plain that their existence depended on the sanction of a greater authority. St. Paul, for example, recognizes, so far as one may judge, no legitimate structure within the churches such as to limit either the degree or the manner of his own authority over the churches. Apostolic authority is to any lesser authority in the New Testament churches as substance is to shadow. Therefore the question arises whether in this Apostolic authority which stands over against all the aspirations of the local congregations, founding and controlling the church, judging and sanctioning, exhorting and reprimanding—the question arises whether we have here at least the type of something essential to the life of the church, which is now permanently represented in the historic episcopate; or whether, on the other hand, such authority was a temporary necessity, to be discarded or diffused as the church grew, through experience and precedent, into wisdom and stability.

In support of the former alternative, much has been made

of our Lord's choice of, and injunctions to, the Twelve. We shall return to this point; here we need only take note of the claim that, in the commissioning of the Twelve, our Lord's constitution of an authority was prior to his constitution of a church. An authority to act in his name, to stand in the same relationship to him as that in which he stands to the Father—this, it is claimed, is our Lord's first appointment; and so far from this authority being but a passing necessity in the life of the church, it is in fact around and upon this authority that the church first comes into being and thereafter lives. That all Christians are to do Christ's work is, of course, in a general sense true; but there is a narrower and more precise sense in which His work is committed to the few. There is a commission which extends not to the whole body of Christian people nor to the leaders chosen by the members from among that body, but to a limited and well defined group which is prior to that body; and this limited commission bears, in a quite unique sense, Christ's own authority.

In as far as this claim rests upon a particular method of New Testament interpretation, we shall return to it later. In so far as it rests upon the straightforward meaning of the words of the Lord, it cannot be taken as proven. The point is not of the authority which the Lord committed to His church as such, but of that which He committed to the Twelve as the constitutive nucleus, with an authority distinct from and prior to the common voice of the church. This being so, such a passage as Matt. xviii. 18—'whatsoever ye shall bind on earth shall be bound in heaven'—is not to the point, since the audience to which it is addressed is simply specified as the 'disciples'. The passage occurs in what is apparently a collection of more or less detached sayings of the Lord; and if it should be argued that originally it was addressed to the Twelve alone, yet the fact remains that the Evangelist omits this limited reference. He is not careful to specify the recipients of such weighty authority: he seems unaware of any distinction such as that postulated by the present theory between the authority of the church as a whole and that of the Twelve within and over the church. It is true that in Matt. xvi. 19 the Evangelist attributes this same power of binding and loosing to St. Peter, as the Rock on which the church shall stand. It appears at first sight that St. Peter, possibly as an individual, but possibly also as the leader and spokesman of the Twelve, is invested with a quite distinctive authority; but the later reference, in which identical authority is attributed to a wider and apparently unrestricted circle, must warn against pursuing the former too closely. St. Matthew knows the authority of the church; he knows the authority of him who, presiding over the church, speaks in the name of the church; he knows no distinctive and restricted authority prior to the church, constitutive of it and dominant over it.

Another important saying of the Lord, 'as my Father hath sent me, even so send I you', is not specified by the Fourth Evangelist as limited to the Twelve, although the context makes such a restricted reference possible. In any case, such pregnant words should not be narrowed down to some such signification as 'in sending you I invest you with that authority with which the Father has invested me'. It is equally likely that Our Lord was not so much investing the Twelve with authority as enjoining upon them loyalty and obedience: 'as I have done the Father's will, so shall ye do mine'. Again, 'he that receiveth you receiveth me; and he that receiveth me receiveth him that sent me': but the 'little ones' are to be received as Christ no less than the Twelve; and to assert, as Dr. Farrer does in the 'Apostolic Ministry', that whereas the 'little ones' are to be received for the reason of their suffering humanity, the Twelve are to be received on the grounds of their divine commission—this is to make a distinction of which our Lord himself seems wholly unaware. It is not by such strained interpretation of isolated sayings of our Lord that we shall understand the nature of his commission, but only in the light of the actual claims and conduct of those who, having received themselves his commission, were in the best position to perceive its meaning.

On this principle, the account of the election of Matthias to the number of the Twelve is of importance. Whether or not it is a perfectly accurate account of the facts, it is the account of one who presumably knew what the Twelve were, and what they understood themselves to be. As to any authority of any kind which Matthias is to exercise, the account is silent; as to his function it is perfectly plain. He is to be a witness of the Resurrection; and since the testimony which he is to bear—the testimony which appears in the pattern of the primitive kerygma—is a testimony not simply to the Resurrection but to him who rose again, and includes some reference to the work of his ministry, the chosen witness is to be one of those who were with the Lord continuously during the years of his ministry. That 'we are witnesses to these things' is as consistently proclaimed in the early apostolic preaching as is the message of the Resurrection itself (Acts ii. 32; iii. 15; v. 32; x. 39); that 'we are the heirs of his authority' or that 'we are the princes of his kingdom' is a claim conspicuous by its absence in the earliest days of the Church.

After the election of Matthias, the Twelve, as such, virtually disappear from history. If their primary function was that of proclaiming a first hand and authentic testimony, this further development is not surprising. Their work, as the Twelve, was soon done. The message which they announced was bound to become common knowledge at least in the immediate vicinity; and once a story is well-known, the testimony of an eyewitness is unnecessary among those who are ready to receive it, and ineffective among those who are not. Even had they wished to do so, the Twelve could not possibly have confined the preaching of the Gospel to themselves. Although their status as the original Twelve, the primary witnesses, was remembered and respected in later years, their function would become less distinctive as others took up, repeated and passed on their testimony. It would not be necessary, as death took its toll, to incorporate others to fill up the gaps among the Twelve; nor, as the years passed by, would it be easy to find others with the qualifications originally required of Matthias. The gradual disappearance of the Twelve in their distinctive function is, on this hypothesis, only to be expected. But if, on the other hand, the Twelve were, and understood themselves to be, the chosen and exclusive heirs of dominical authority, the later development is hard indeed to understand. The need for a decisive authority within the church clearly did not diminish in the New Testament period, and the Twelve were the obvious and, indeed, the inevitable seat and source of authority; and yet in fact, within a very few years, we find the guiding authority of the church resting not with the Twelve as such, nor only with the Twelve; and the title which ought, on this hypothesis, to have been the very touchstone of the delegated authority of the Lord, virtually disappears from history. If, in view of the increase of the Church, it became necessary to increase the number of authoritative offices within the church, the obvious course would be to delegate authority downwards, so creating a pyramidal structure, with a self-perpetuating order of Twelve at the apex. To broaden the structure of authority laterally, to set others, however chosen, on a par with the original heirs of the Lord's authority; to abandon, for all practical purposes, the honoured title of the Twelve and to class together, under the common title of Apostle, the survivors of the original Twelve and their later associates or delegates—this would be strange behaviour indeed had the Twelve so understood their office as this theory requires.

It does not, then, seem true that the Twelve understood their Lord's call and injunctions as, primarily, the delegation of authority. And this being so, it does not carry the argument much further to attempt to prove that all others who shared with the Twelve the title and authority of Apostle had either received a call from the Lord as objective and unambiguous as that of the Twelve to the Mountain, or had been directly commissioned by the Twelve. If St. Paul believed that his call on the Damascus road conferred upon him, or made him heir to, the Lord's own authority, then he must have believed more than the Twelve believed of their own call. In any case, St. Paul—and he is the only one among the Apostles whom we see in the actual exercise of his authority—does not seem to have believed this. On what does St. Paul base his claim to be heard and his demand for obedience? There is no single answer. Where he is answering the contention that his authority, being derivative, is there-

fore subordinate, he naturally points to the immediate en-
counter on the Damascus road as the source of his authority
and, incidentally, of his Gospel also (Gal. i. 1 and 12). But
at other times his claim to be heard rests on the conformity
of his teaching to the accepted and universal tradition of the
church (1 Cor. xiii, 36: xv. 1 ff.): it is the content of the
preaching which guarantees the status of the preacher, and
not the status of the preacher which validates the preaching
—'if even we, or even an angel from heaven, should preach
to you a Gospel other than that which we have preached,
let him be anathema' (Gal. i. 8). Elsewhere St. Paul claims
that although his counsel 'concerning the Virgins' (1 Cor.
vii. 25 and 40) has not the decisive authority of a commandment of the Lord, it must yet receive respect as the opinion
of one 'found faithful by the Lord' who thinks that he also
'has the spirit of the Lord'. Elsewhere again it is the possession by the Apostle of an authentic 'word of the Lord', possibly unknown to his readers, which vindicates some particular aspect of his teaching (1 Thess. iv. 15; 1 Cor. vii. 10).
In other instances, *vis-à-vis* the church of Corinth, St. Paul
rests his authority on his special position as the 'founding
father' of the Church (1 Cor. iv, 15; 2 Cor. x. 14). Finally, in
the latter part of 2 Corinthians, in the refutation of the
sharpest challenge to his authority, St. Paul defends his
position by an argument which he himself condemns as
'fleshly' but which he appears all the same to consider
relevant; and this is an argument based on his primacy in
service and suffering and on the charismatic vindication of
his Apostolate (2 Cor. xi. 16 ff.; xii. 12). With all this evidence before us, we cannot posit, in the early church, any
single, clear-cut and decisive theory of the grounds of
Apostolic authority. No such theory was known to St. Paul
or accepted by those to whom he wrote. It would be nearer
the truth to say that it is the Apostle's burning sense of
responsibility for the Gospel which drives him, inevitably, to
the exercise of authority; he requires the authority which
will secure a hearing for the Gospel and which, in this form-
ative stage of the church, will call forth a faithful obedience
to its precepts, and he grounds the authority which he re-

quires on several different aspects of his Christian experience.

Thus while it may be argued that the recognition of a single focus of authority is necessary in practice at all times to the church's functioning, it does not appear from the New Testament that it is also essential in theory to the church's being. It would appear that in so far as St. Paul's authority rested upon his personal position as founder and father of the Corinthian church, it died with him; that in so far as it rested upon his service and suffering, it passed to those of whatever age and status who have laboured as he did; that in so far as it rested upon the purity of his Gospel, it passed into the written Scriptures. When all has been said on the decisiveness of Apostolic authority in the early church, it falls short of establishing, as the essential core and centre of the church, the presence of inherited dominical authority.

We must now turn to a rather different line of argument, according to which the episcopate is understood as that which bears the substance of the church. Episcopacy is not simply a particularly ancient and effective form of church order; nor is it, primarily, the medium through which divine authority is communicated to the church. The typical function of the Bishop is neither to organize nor to command; it is simply 'to be the Bishop'—for, as Ignatius said, where he is, there is the church. The key-word in this argument is not 'authority' but 'hierarchy'; and the central concept which governs the nature of the church is that of the Kingdom—of the society whose being is determined by its order. It is the hierarchical structure which constitutes the Kingdom, and which therefore, on this view, determined the church; where the episcopate is, and there only, is the Kingdom. A group of well-wishers of the Kingdom, however well organized, however sympathetic to its aims and receptive of its principles, does not, in itself, constitute the Kingdom or any part of it. Such a group may display all the attributes of the church; but it *is* the church only if it bears within itself the essential substance transmitted through the historic episcopate.

Stated in such a form, this argument appears far removed from the immediacy of New Testament thought and expression. But it is, as a matter of fact, from the New Testament itself that its guiding principles are derived. The New Testament, it is alleged, rings with echoes of the Old too subtle for immediate perception by our relatively unattuned ears; it is replete with images which, to those who first wrote and read, had profound and far-reaching evocative power; apparently casual phrases and apparently strained analogies opened up vistas of memory and association. New Testament thought continually drives the attentive reader back to particular contexts of the Old Testament, through which the apparent indefiniteness of some New Testament passage is crystallized and defined. Evocations of the Old Israel sharpen, and add precision to, the outlines of the New. And the destiny of the Old Israel was to be, in order and history, the bearer of the divine to mankind. As the individual Israelite became an Israelite through the form of circumcision, so Israel became Israel through the Law: the being of the society as a whole was constituted by the Law— a Law of hierarchy and ritual no less than of morality. The ideal of a hierarchial order, of a society which in every detail of its structure is instinct with the divine, was that towards which the Old Israel tended; and therefore, the more consistently the story of the New Israel is written and read in terms of the Old, the more prominent here also will be the idea of a grace-bearing order, of hierarchy in the fullest sense, of an essential and constitutive structure. The typological interpretation of the New Testament tends in general towards the interpretation of the Church in terms of structure rather than of spirit.

How far is this method legitimate? That it may be pushed to extravagant lengths is evident; the study of subtle and even half unconscious evocations can hardly proceed by rigid canons of objectivity. But abuse in its application does not invalidate a method in itself; it is not enough to bring the charge of subjectivity against the typological method. The real criticism lies deeper.

We know that among the leading preoccupations of the New Testament writers, and of the Apostolic preachers before them, was that of discovering in the words and deeds of

Jesus of Nazareth significance and fulfilment. That all had happened according to the Scriptures was the most powerful proof that he who was known as a carpenter and condemned as a criminal was not simply a good man and a great teacher but, in the full and final sense, 'He that should come'. It is clear, for instance, that for the Evangelists the Twenty-second Psalm was fulfilled in the Passion of the Lord, so that to some extent the memory of that Psalm has determined the form of the Passion narratives. Many another unquestionable echo of the Old Testament comes to mind by which the New Testament writers gave substance to their conviction that 'this is very Christ'.

But the fact is that he who came according to the Scriptures was rejected by those who claimed to be expert in the Scriptures. For in the fulfilment of the Scriptures there was also a transcending or transvaluation of the Scriptures; so that to human wisdom untransformed by grace his Person remained opaque and his claims scandalous. The Jews as well as the Greeks fell under St. Paul's condemnation that 'the world in its wisdom knew not God'; and thus 'the foolishness of the preaching' is antithetical not only to the philosophy of the Greek, but also to the biblicism of the Jew. The Christian recognizes the types of Christ and his Kingdom in the Old Testament not through a technical wisdom superior to that of the unconverted Jew, but through a distinctive mode of understanding which, in relation to that of the Jew, must appear as paradoxical. Thus, from the point of view of Christian theology, any simple extrapolation of Old Testament concepts into the New is excluded in principle; and to the contention that the Old Testament is reflected in the New, we must add the qualification that this reflection is, in some sense, inverted, as the reflection of a landscape in a lake. The Old Testament images detected in the New must be transformed by the paradox of a crucified Messiah before they can become definitive for Christian theology.

What such transformation means, or at least what it may mean, can be illustrated from our Lord's injunctions to the Twelve. It is obviously probable that the number Twelve recalled, and was intended to recall, the ancient patriarchs and tribal princes of Israel; the Twelve of the New Kingdom were to correspond in some sense to the patriarchs and princes of the Old. So in the eschatological fulfilment, when the Son of Man shall sit in glory, they also shall be enthroned as judges of the Kingdom. At first sight this is a promise that the New Kingdom also shall contain a pattern of hierarchy, with authority, and the magnificent symbols of authority, for those who are granted pre-eminence; and that such pre-eminence shall belong to the Twelve. But, as appears from the context of the relevant passages both in St. Matthew and St. Luke, this interpretation involves a mistaken emphasis, which, in certain circumstances, may be as misleading as a direct falsehood. The point is not that the New Kingdom shall mirror the order of the Old, though with new names inscribed upon the foremost thrones; it is rather that the New Kingdom shall so invert the order of the Old that pre-eminence belongs where it would least be expected — to those who have abandoned all place and claim to place, and have followed the Lord through his tribulations. The primacy of the New Kingdom is an essentially paradoxical primacy; until the Eschaton itself, it is unmarked save by the inverted symbols of service, humility and having-no-place; and lest anyone should reassure himself that, having taken the lowest place here, he shall have the highest hereafter, there remains the further paradox that the first shall be last and the last first. So also, when the dispute arises over pre-eminence among the Twelve and our Lord contrasts the principles that are to apply among them with the principles of the rulers of the Gentiles, the presupposition of his words is not, as Dr. Farrer says, that 'with whatever humility, they are to rule' (op. cit., p. 121). If this were the case, it could mean, in terms of the comparison, that some of the Twelve are to rule *others of the Twelve*, though in a spirit opposed to that in which Gentile rulers rule their subjects; which is clearly not the point which the Lord was making. In any case, he had a sharper contrast to draw than that between ruling tyrannically and ruling with humility: as a matter of fact he makes no mention of the methods by which the Gentile rulers acquire and exercise power. His contrast is between ruling

35

by whatever means and not ruling at all, but rather serving. He says to the whole band what he says in effect to James and John—that he has in his Kingdom no titles of honour or authority to assign, but only a share in his own title and office of *diaconos*.

Our Lord's call of a group to the particular number of Twelve, and his solemn and formal method of calling, which may again have Old Testament associations, reveal the measure and stature of what he was doing. His action constitutes a New Israel, and so belies the interpretation of his work in general as simply a reforming movement within the Old Israel or a reassumption of the prophetic office. It indicates the dimensions of his person and his work, but it says nothing, if we may so put it, of the distinctive content which lies within these dimensions. We take it as a general principle that the quotation—direct and indirect—of the Old Testament within the New, and the assimilation of New Testament language and images to Old Testament types—we take it that this points to the *fact* of fulfilment in Jesus as the Christ, but not to the paradoxical *form* in which the fulfilment tends to appear.

This principle sets a limit to the typological interpretation of the New Testament. The typological method reinforces our conviction that the event of Christ was interpreted by our Lord himself and his immediate followers as no simple historical event, however wonderful, but as the very centre and climax of history; but the method does not directly illuminate the meaning of this event in terms of life, conduct and function to those who receive it as the centre of history. It is not necessarily true that, because the being of the Old Israel was determined by an essential structure, so also is that of the New.

Yet the question of structure is still of cardinal importance to the present enquiry. The episcopate is clearly the keystone of ecclesiastical structure, and controversy over the meaning of episcopacy is important precisely because it involves the whole relationship between structure and spirit in the life of the Church. Generally speaking, this relationship is represented in one of two ways. On the one hand, structure is represented as determinative of spirit; spirit is mediated through, and only through, an essential structure. The presence of that structure is the guarantee of the presence of the Spirit: 'where the Bishop is, there is the Church'. Where we find the Church, as defined in structural terms, we shall expect also the manifestation of the Spirit in terms of love, joy, peace and the other virtues; but where there is no evident manifestation of the Spirit, we shall not immediately question the validity of the structure. It will be a matter of faith that, beyond what is apparent on the surface, the Spirit is nevertheless present and at work. On the other hand, the Spirit may be represented as determinative of ecclesiastical structure; it is the manifestation of the Spirit which validates any particular form of structure. Where the fruits of the Spirit are manifest, there is the church; the proper order for the Church in any particular age or circumstance is that which is most effectively and powerfully revealing the presence of the Spirit.

These two points of view are, despite their antithesis, alike in one respect. In each case structure is represented as the *vehicle or medium* of the Spirit. In the first case, we start with the given structure, and look for the manifestation of the Spirit in and through it. In the second case, we start with the fruits of the Spirit, and look for that structural form through which, in a particular age, they are most powerfully manifested. The accepted structure will be, in either case, the bearer of the Spirit.

But is this the New Testament point of view? We must note, first, that in the majority of images under which the Church is represented a structural form is apparent—the Body, the Building, the Vine, the Temple. The Church is not a mere plenum, but an articulated whole; it is not, for example, expressed in such metaphors as a River of righteousness or a New Flood cleansing the world from sin or as a purifying Wind. The preference is for images drawn from those realities in which we can see, as it were, behind the matter of the reality, an articulated form or skeleton or framework. Yet we must not think of this form in static terms, as an existing entity upon which the matter of the

37

Church simply coagulates. 'The whole building,' says the writer to the Ephesians, 'fitly framed together *is growing into* a holy temple in the Lord, in which you also *are being built together* for the purpose of a dwelling place of God in the Spirit' (Eph. ii. 21–2). 'The whole body . . . *is making* its proper growth into the building up of itself in love' (Eph. iv. 16). The purpose of the diversified ministries ordained by the Spirit is '*unto* the building of the Body of Christ', '*unto* unity of faith and knowledge of the Son of God', '*unto* the perfect man' (Eph. iv. 11 ff.). The Church *is* the Body of Christ; yet even this metaphor does not point to a reality which is formally complete, and incapable of the degrees of 'more' or 'less'; for, as the Body of Christ, the Church is a fullness or completion *towards* which the Christ Himself grows (Eph. i. 23). The principle on which, according to St. Paul, the various charismatic gifts are to be evaluated and exercised is that of 'edification'; but this word has become too colourless to carry the significance of the original word *oikodome*. The Spirit is given not for private edification in the conventional sense of the term, but 'for the building up' of an organic and integrated whole, for the creation of a reality which shall express, in its integrated diversity, both the oneness and the manifold richness of the Spirit.

Thus structure emerges not as the medium or vehicle of the Spirit, but as the expression or embodiment of the Spirit. The Spirit embodies itself, more or less fully, in a meaningful structure. This point of view becomes even clearer when we consider the ultimate purpose of the church. The writer to the Ephesians is perhaps the first of the New Testament theologians to focus his attention upon the historical progress of the church and its supra-historical destiny: he looks beyond his own epoch in the church's life, beyond its contemporary triumphs and tragedies, beyond the transformations effected by it in individual lives; he has in mind a clear answer to the question, 'When all this has been achieved, when all the elect have been gathered in, when the church is a glorious church "without spot or blemish or anything such", what then is its ultimate purpose?' In the magnificent perspective of this Epistle, there is one dominant and all-embracing end to which the being of the church and even the perfecting of the church is subservient; and this end, in the phrase which occurs three times within the first few verses of the Epistle, is 'the praise of the glory of God'. The church is to shew what God has done; men and angels, looking upon the church, are to see what God has done; and seeing, they will be moved to praise Him for His wisdom and goodness (Eph. iii. 10: ii, 7). The church is to be the ever-present reality which shall make plain, within history and beyond history, God's work of redemption, and so shall elicit, from the choirs of heaven and earth, the praise of his wisdom and His goodness.

It is commonly taught that the Christian, in his individual moral life, is to live to the glory of God. His moral conduct is not to be determined by the fear of punishment and the quest of reward. Rather it is to be the natural and inevitable expression of the Risen Life in which he shares. So, living as one who is 'risen with Christ', the Christian will indeed live to the glory of God: he will, as it were, point beyond himself to that of which his own life is the expression—to the enduring power of Christ's Risen Life; and those who see will be moved to wonder, not at the perfection of the individual life itself, but at the power and grace of Him who is its source and spring. The Christian lives to the glory of God in so far as he expresses in word and deed the Risen Life in which he shares.

In the same sense, and to the same end, the church is to express in its corporate life the nature and the quality of God's redeeming work. The Spirit embodies itself in structural form. Just as good works are not constitutive but expressive of the Christian character, so episcopacy is not constitutive of the Church but the expression in structural form of the Spirit. Through this structure is to be expressed God's redeeming work. It is as if men and angels, by looking at the church in its structural form no less than in the moral life of its individual members, are to see the nature and meaning of God's act in Christ; and, seeing, are to be moved to wonder and to praise. The church is to be that enclave of

39

contemporary reality in which the grace of God is made evident in a meaningful and expressive form.

Thus we return to the starting point of this essay. The New Testament provides no 'answer' to modern controversy over the nature of episcopacy; but it does provide a context, a guiding principle, within which the historical and philosophical examination of the problem may continue. The episcopate is the keystone of the structural order of the church; and the question of episcopacy is crucial simply because it is the focal point of the significance of structure in and for the life of the church. The New Testament does not point to the idea of a Spirit-bearing structure. The Spirit is not bound; and therefore we must reject, on the one hand, discussion of ecclesiastical structure in terms of validity: we must reject the theory of a single, determinate structure as decisive for the presence of the Spirit and the being of the church. We must reject, on the other hand, discussion of ecclesiastical structure in terms of utility; we must reject the theory of a comparative evaluation of various structural forms in terms of their effectiveness in mediating the fruits of the Spirit. *We are led by the New Testament to discuss the problem of structure in terms neither of validity nor of utility, but of meaning.* The structure of the church is not the medium but the expression of the Spirit. Thus the measure of the fullness of the church is the degree to which it bears witness, in its structural being, to the nature and meaning of God's act of redemption. That the historic episcopate expresses the Christocentric and Christogenetic character of the church, that it points to the divine initiative in our redemption both as a historical and as a contemporary reality, that it creates a formal order of obedience of the church to its Lord—all this can be cogently and convincingly upheld. But it does not follow that the church separated from the episcopate ceases to be the church, that it is deprived of its essential and constitutive structure. Its life is still the life of the Spirit. But it waits for the perfecting of the body, for the amplification of its structure, for the more complete expression in concrete and visible form of its own inner life and meaning.

III

THE MINISTRY AND ORDER
OF THE CHURCH
IN THE WORKS OF THE FATHERS

K. J. Woollcombe

VINCENT OF LÉRINS is remembered for his Canon: 'In the
Catholic Church itself we take the greatest care to hold that
which has been believed everywhere, always and by all.'[1]
He would perhaps have disowned it, if he had foreseen how
it would encourage the habit of speaking of the Fathers as
if they had all lived at the same time in the same place, and
had spoken with the same mind at the same conference
table. For, a little later in the same work, he wrote: 'The
Catholic Christian must do his best to compare the opinions
of the Fathers and enquire their meaning, provided always
that, though they belonged to diverse times and places, they
yet continued in the Faith of the One Catholic Church, and
were approved and outstanding teachers. And whatever he
shall find to have been held, written and taught, not by one
or two only, but by all equally and with one consent, openly,
frequently and persistently, let him take this as to be held
by him without the slightest hesitation.'[2] The Fathers did
not all teach the same doctrine of the Historic Episcopate
equally, openly, frequently and persistently; let us be sure
of not asking them questions about it as if they had. Neither
let us expect them to offer a solution to our problems; theirs
were quite different.

Instead let us acknowledge that the Fathers were, for the
most part, practical men, seeking reasonable and tolerant
solutions to problems of Church Order as they arose in the
context of many different kinds of schism and disorder. The

---

[1] *Commonitorium* 2. PL. 50. 640.
[2] *ib.* 3. PL. 50. 641.

solutions differed widely according to the situation of the Fathers—an African schism responded to one kind of treatment, an Asiatic to another; they differed too according to the temperament and, let us admit it, the temper of the Fathers—one so diplomatic as Cyprian will not readily agree with one so cantankerous as Stephen. Nevertheless they were honest attempts to solve extremely difficult problems, and they were all made in order to preserve the wholeness of the Body of Christ, and to give it an order and orderliness worthy of so great a name.

It was to correct a lack of orderliness in the Church of Corinth that Clement wrote to the Corinthians at the close of the first century. His Epistle is the first extant document on Church Order, but it is *a letter*, not a theological treatise. Clement pleads with the members of the Church of Corinth to be as lowly-minded as were the Patriarchs and Prophets of old. 'For Christ is with them that are lowly of mind, not with them that exalt themselves over the flock' (16). Only upon the humble does God confer the benefits of peace and order which characterize His Universe (20). Moreover, it is God's will that His peace and order should be maintained by a Ministry of His own making. 'The Apostles received the Gospel for us from the Lord Jesus Christ; Jesus Christ was sent forth from God. So then Christ is from God, and the Apostles are from Christ. Both therefore came of the will of God in the appointed order. Having therefore received a charge, and having been fully assured through the Resurrection of Our Lord Jesus Christ and confirmed in the word of God with full assurance of the Holy Ghost, they went forth with the glad tidings that the Kingdom of God should come. So preaching everywhere in country and town, they appointed their first fruits, when they had proved them by the Holy Spirit, to be Bishops and Deacons unto them that should believe' (42). Such a ministry is no new remedy against disorder. Moses, foreseeing that the question of succession to the priesthood would arouse jealousy, received the commandment of God to invest Aaron and his descendants with the rights of the priesthood (Num. 17). So 'our Apostles knew through Our Lord Jesus Christ that there would be strife over the name of the Bishop's office. For this cause therefore, having received complete foreknowledge, they appointed the aforesaid persons, and afterwards they made an enactment, that if these men should fall asleep, other "approved" men *the big ?* should succeed to their ministration. Those therefore who were appointed by them, or afterward by other men of repute with the consent of the whole church, and have ministered unblameably to the flock of Christ in lowliness of mind . . . these men we consider to be unjustly thrust out from their ministration. For it will be no light sin for us if we thrust out from the bishop's office those who have *offered the gifts*[1] unblameably and holily' (44).

Clement's writing at this crucial point of his rather long-winded epistle is admittedly obscure, but his main contention is clear: 'It is essential to the well-being and good order of the Church, that approved men should succeed to the ministration (*leitourgia*) of the Apostles'. The Apostles founded churches and appointed bishops and deacons to minister to them. At first it seemed that the Second Coming of Christ might take place before all the Apostles died, but time went on, and the Apostles did die. Yet their ministry—their *lei-tourgia*—had to go on, and so other approved men were appointed, either by the Apostles (following Dix)[2], or by the bishops (following Lightfoot), to succeed to it.

We must not be misled into thinking that Clement was speaking of a continuance of the Apostolate (whatever that may mean). Clement did not think in terms of 'Apostolate' or 'Episcopate'—he thought in terms of men who were Apostles or bishops. He was concerned only with the continuance of what they did—their ministration. The question is: Did the *leitourgia* of the Apostles differ from that of the bishops? Dom Gregory Dix thought it did; he says that the *leitourgia* of the Apostles was the appointment of local episcopoi and diaconoi.[3] The *leitourgia* of the episcopoi, whatever it may have been, did not include that. *Leitourgia*, however, is a word, which, as Dix admits,[4] was used in the

---

[1] The modern equivalent of this would be '*celebrated the Holy Eucharist*'.
[2] *The Apostolic Ministry*, pp. 285 ff.
[3] *ib.* p. 262.
[4] *ib.* p. 194.

43

LXX to convey the meaning of *ministration* 'on behalf of the community, with special reference to the divinely ordered and organized worship of the Temple cultus at Jerusalem'.[1] When, therefore, the Apostolic Fathers began to use the word to describe the *ministration* of the Apostles and bishops, they had in mind their special privilege of offering the Eucharistic gifts on behalf of the community.[2] Beside this privileged ministration, any other ministration would have seemed but a small thing, and it would have been considered only sensible and practical to have provided for its continuance. There is indeed nothing in Clement's letter to suggest that he thought that the Eucharistic *leitourgia* was one ministration, and the appointment of successors to it, another. In Clement's mind the one and only *leitourgia* is the Eucharistic *leitourgia*, and the appointment of successors to it is a matter of common sense. In Dom Gregory Dix's view, however, the bishops' *leitourgia* did not include the right of appointing their own successors, whereas the Apostles' *leitourgia* did. This seems to me to make an unnatural distinction in Clement's use of the word, which is manifestly uniform throughout the passage in question. It is surely more natural to suppose that, if the Apostles were determined to ensure the continuance of the Eucharistic *leitourgia*, they would not have appointed successors with limited powers. The Apostles were not numerous, they travelled widely, and were not in telegraphic communication with the churches they founded. To have provided for a 'second-fruits' ministry to succeed to the first, which they founded on the spot, would have been a geographical impossibility. The most the Apostles could have done, was to have insisted that approved men should succeed to the *leitourgia* which they had bestowed upon the first *episcopoi*.[3] They could not

---

[1] In the N.T. the word *leitourgia* was not restricted to the context of the *worship* of the Christian community, cf. 2 Cor. 9: 12., Phil. 2: 17, 30. But in the Epistle of Clement, it was beginning to be so restricted, v.s.v. *leitourgia*, Strathmann ap. Kittel TWNT.

[2] vid. sup. p. 43. Clem. *ep.* 44, 'those who have offered the gifts'.

[3] The story of Apollos (Acts 18: 24 ff.) is an example of this. According to Clement, Apollos was a man 'approved' (*dedokimasmenos*) by the Apostles (47. 4). Now, if the story in Acts is right, Apollos was instructed by Priscilla and Aquila (who had been with St. Paul at Corinth), approved by the brethren at Ephesus (*not* by St. Paul), and sent by them on a mission to Corinth. That his intention

themselves have appointed this second generation of the ministry, since they would not have been on the spot—they could only require the episcopoi to *approve* their successors, just as they had been approved by the Apostles.

Let us summarize the stages in the formation of the ministry as Clement sees them:

1. The Apostles founded churches.
2. They appointed a first-fruits ministry of bishops and deacons approved by the Spirit.
3. They left the churches to fend for themselves and went away to found others.
4. In course of time some of the Apostles died, and so did some members of the first-fruits ministry.
5. The remainder of the Apostles made an enactment that approved men should always offer the Eucharistic gifts, and provided for the orderly succession of that privilege.
6. As necessary, approved men were appointed, either by the Apostles, or by whoever happened to be on the spot who had succeeded to the Apostles' *leitourgia*.[1]

Dom Gregory Dix held that if we supposed the first episcopoi to have recruited men to their own ministry, we should, in the first place, 'make nonsense of Clement's insistence (43 and 44.1) on the Apostles' foreknowledge that there would be strife about the name of the episcope.[2] In spite of this divinely given foreknowledge, they had deliberately done away with their own precautions against such strife just when their own guiding hand was about to be removed.' Secondly, Dix writes, 'The Apostolic "enactment" was not carried out. Episcopoi in the second century received their katastasis not from their own church, but, as in the Apostolic Age, still from outside it, by consecration at the hands of bishops from elsewhere.'

---

was to continue the work of St. Paul is clear from 1 Cor. 3: 6, 'I planted, Apollos watered'. It would be incredible if this had not included Baptism, Preaching and the Eucharist, since these were precisely the difficulties on which St. Paul had later to give advice (1 Cor. 1: 12–17; 2; 11: 17 ff.).

[1] No reference has here been made to the Epistles of Ignatius, since we have a more crucial difficulty to examine in the Epistle of Clement. It is, however, the Eucharistic *leitourgia* of the Bishop which is of primary importance in the Ignatian Epistles.

[2] op. cit., p. 261.

Let us take the second of Dom Gregory Dix's points first. In the *Second Century* episcopoi of course received katastasis from outside bishops. By that time monepiscopacy had been established, and when the sole bishop of a church died, his successor *had* to be consecrated by an outside bishop. But in the *First Century*, before the advent of monepiscopacy, there was no need for this procedure, since there were other bishops locally available; and there is certainly no evidence that it ever took place. As regards his first point: it seems to me that Dom Gregory Dix failed to see what was the essential feature of the Apostles' precautions against strife about the name of the episcope. He thought that the continuance of the Apostolate by the Apostles was the precaution they intended. But, surely, even if this had been geographically possible, it was not what Clement wrote. In his letter the emphasis is all on the succession of *approved men with the consent of the Church*. It was quite a sufficient guarantee of the continuance of an orderly ministry, that only men whose work for Christ had been manifestly blessed by the Spirit should succeed to the episcopate, with the consent of the whole church.[1] In Corinth, lawless and unruly men, whose work for Christ had manifestly *not* been blessed by the Spirit, had succeeded to the episcopate *without* the consent of the church—that is the *raison d'être* of Clement's letter. 'Those, therefore, who were appointed by them or afterward by other men of repute (*ellogimoi andres*)[2] with the consent of the whole Church ... these men we consider to be unjustly thrust out from their ministration.'

The Epistle of Clement offers no solution to the present problem of Church Order in South India, but it does point to some features of that problem which are too often over-

[1] It has always been a rule of the Church that the election of a bishop should take place with the public consent of the clergy and laity. *See* Hippolytus, Apostolic Tradition. 2. 2. ed. Dix p. 3. Cited, *The Apostolic Ministry*, p. 196.

[2] The root meaning of *ellogimos* is *enrolled* in a list or in an account; in later Greek it meant little more than *wise*. To render *ellogimoi andres*, with Dix, *men accounted apostles* is to stretch the meaning beyond its natural extent. Clement *may* simply have meant that the Apostles' successors were wise men. If, on the other hand, he meant that they were enrolled in a list, they could certainly have been enrolled in the list of bishops without being accounted as Apostles. Indeed Clement, in common with the earliest Fathers, puts the Apostles in a class by themselves (5).

looked. Clement would insist that the Apostolic *leitourgia* must continue in the Church of South India, and that successors to it must be men whose work for Christ is already manifestly approved by the Spirit, appointed with the consent of the whole church. The unanimity of the C.S.I. and its numerous and manifest blessings from the Holy Spirit would carry far more weight with Clement than the fact that all its ministers are not yet within the tactual line of Apostolic Succession.

It is clear from Clement's Epistle that disorders and schisms rent the Church asunder long before the Fathers had thought out what repercussions they might have upon other doctrines, such as the doctrines of the Ministry and the Holy Eucharist. Consequently, when we consider what the Fathers have to say about schism and its effect upon the validity of orders, we have to remember that they were not primarily dealing with problems of doctrine, but with problems of discipline and organization. These problems usually arose during outbreaks of violent persecution, which gave the Fathers little time to think and few opportunities to confer with each other. The marvellous thing is that, although they had to make rapid decisions to keep the Christian communities together, they seldom made rash decisions, and were anxious that the solutions which they proposed for the solution of their own local problems should also be acceptable to the Catholic Church as a whole.

I believe then that the most important advice the Fathers have to give us to-day is something like this: 'You have various situations to deal with, arising out of schism. So did we: we had the Melitian schism of Alexandria, the Meletian schism of Antioch, the Novatianist schism of Rome and the Donatist schism of Africa. Ambrose had to do something about the clergy ordained by his Arian predecessor, Auxentius of Milan; the Spanish Church had to do something about the Arianism of the Barbarian invaders. We never found simple or universal answers to these problems; we do not expect that you will; we do not even expect to be of much help to you, because our problems were so different. But we

D

do expect you to base everything you think and do upon the necessity of preserving the wholeness of the Catholic Church —the Body of Christ.'

Let us now press them for information in certain particulars: for instance the question of Apostolic Succession. Hegesippus and Irenaeus had introduced the idea of the Bishop's succession in office as the guarantee of the truth of what he preached. Only the bishops who could trace the unbroken succession of their office from the Apostles could claim Apostolic authority—'with the succession of the episcopate they received the assured gift of truth'.[1] Irenaeus, of course, intended thereby to refute the Gnostics' claim to a secret store of hitherto unrevealed truth. But the Doctrine of Apostolic Succession became a stock weapon in the Apologist's armoury, and Optatus of Milev used it to refute the claim of the Donatist Macrobius to be the rightful Bishop of Rome.[2] It is, however, important to remember that the Early Fathers always taught that Apostolic Succession depended on the fact of the ordination of a successor to a vacant see; they seldom commented on the status of the administrators of the rite of consecration. Nobody ever questioned the Apostolicity of the See of Alexandria, and Egyptian bishops regarded themselves as within the Apostolic Succession,[3] yet it appears that the Popes of Alexandria were consecrated by the College of Presbyters until the Council of Nicaea in A.D. 325.

Dr. Telfer has recently set out all the evidence for the procedure which the early Alexandrine Church followed when a new Bishop was elected and consecrated.[4] He argues that in the earliest days, it is likely that bishops were elected *and* consecrated by their fellow-presbyters. Irenaeus can only have been consecrated to succeed the martyred Pothinus of Lyons by his fellow-presbyters. The Bishops of Rome were probably consecrated in the same way at least until the middle

---

[1] cum episcopatus successione, charisma veritatis certum . . . acceperunt. Iren. *haer.* 4. 26. 2 (PG. 7 (1). 1053C).
[2] 2. 3, 4 (PL. 11. 948 ff).
[3] 'Make this man a real bishop, a holy bishop in true succession from the holy Apostles', Serapion. *Euchologion.* 28.
[4] *Episcopal Succession in Egypt.* JEH. Vol. 3. No. 1. April 1952, pp. 1–13.

of the second century.[1] By the end of the second century, however, this practice had in general given way to the received practice of consecration by one or more consecrated bishops. But at Alexandria, according to Jerome, the primitive practice prevailed until the time of Heraclas and Dionysius (A.D. 247). 'For at Alexandria from the days of Mark the Evangelist down to the episcopates of Heraclas and Dionysius, the presbyters used always to nominate one whom they chose out of their own number and set in higher rank'.[2] Severus of Antioch (A.D. 518) gives some support to Jerome's statement—'The Bishop also of the city renowned for its orthodox faith, the city of the Alexandrines, was in old times appointed by presbyters. But in modern times in accordance with the canon which has prevailed everywhere, the solemn institution of their bishop is performed by bishops.'[3]

It makes no difference to the Patristic doctrine of Apostolic Succession if Jerome and Severus are right or wrong, since the Fathers taught that Apostolic Succession depends on the fact of the ordination of a successor to a vacant see. But, if they are right, the modern idea of an unbroken series of bishops, consecrated by bishops, stands condemned. Bishop Gore tried to prove that they were mistaken,[4] and Dom Gregory Dix also found himself unable to believe that such an irregular practice would have escaped the comment of Clement or Origen.[5] But Jerome, in spite of his 'Presbyterian' prejudices, is not likely to have stated a rumour as a fact, or to have invented the theory that the primitive practice lasted a hundred years longer in Alexandria than anywhere else. He would have been too easily found out. Dr. Telfer is convinced that Jerome's statement is true, and believes that the majority of modern scholars share his conviction. He suggests that the consecration of the Monophysite Patriarch Theodosius at the hands of the corpse of his pre-

[1] J. Zeiller. *Histoire de l'Eglise.* ed. Fliche et Martin. Tome 1., p. 377.
[2] Nam et Alexandriae a Marco evangelista usque ad Heraclam et Dionysium episcopos, presbyteri semper unum ex se electum, in excelsiori gradu collocatum, episcopum nominabant. *Ep.* 146 *ad Evang.* (PL. 22. 1194A).
[3] *The Sixth Book of the Select Letters.* Vol. 2. Part 1. p. 213. ed. E. W. Brooks. Text and Translation Society Publications. 1902.
[4] JTS. Vol. 3 (1902). pp. 278–282.
[5] *The Apostolic Ministry.* p. 269. n. 1.

decessor, Timothy III, in February 536, may possibly reflect the ancient manner of consecrating a new Pope.[1] But whatever the manner of electing and consecrating the Alexandrine Bishops may have been, it is most likely to have been brought into conformity with the practice of the rest of Christendom at the Council of Nicaea. The Fourth Canon of Nicaea provides for the future consecration of all bishops at the hands of not less than three *bishops*. Dr. Telfer finds it significant that the Council saw fit to provide only against future irregularities—it made no attempt to regularize the consecration of the Egyptian Bishops already in possession of their sees. Bishops consecrated by previous Popes of Alexandria were regarded as validly consecrated, and as within the Apostolic Succession, since they were accepted by the whole Church as Bishops witnessing to Apostolic Faith and Order, and exercising Apostolic authority.

Let it not be thought that the Fathers of Nicaea were insensitive to such aspects of the doctrine of Holy Orders as concern us to-day—nor that they were likely to overlook any grave irregularities in the administration of the Rites of Ordination. One of the problems on the agenda of the Council was the schism of Melitius, Bishop of Lycopolis. Melitius had invaded the diocese of Thmuis whilst its Bishop, Phileas, was in prison during the persecution of 306, and, without permission, had ordained candidates for the priesthood. After the return of the Patriarch Peter, he was excommunicated for this flagrant breach of Canon Law, whereupon he went into schism and set himself up as the 'orthodox' (i.e. rigorist) Bishop of Alexandria. A little later, during a fresh outbreak of persecution, he was sentenced to be deported to the mines of Phaeno, but he had the good fortune to survive this dreadful punishment, and returned again in 311, after Galerius' Edict of Toleration, to prolong the schism further.

The heresiarch Arius had once been a supporter of

---

[1] Liberatus. *Breviarium*. 20 (PL. 68. 1036–1037A). There is some support for this in the curious seventh-century account of the enthronement of the corpse of Pope Peter. *Sancti Petri Martyris, acta antiqua*. ed. Combefis. *Illustrium Christ Martyrum lecti triumphi*. 1660. pp. 217–220.

Melitius, and had drawn many of his allies from the ranks of the Melitians. It is, therefore, surprising that the Council of Nicaea should have dealt so leniently with the schism. The Synodical Letter[1] merely decreed that, although Melitius was undeserving of pardon, he should only be deprived of the right to exercise episcopal functions; he might retain the honour and title of Bishop, provided he remained in his own city. Those who had been ordained by him were directed to receive a more sacramental ordination (*mystikotera cheirotonia*) in order that they might be confirmed (*bebaiothentes*) in their orders.

It was not uncommon in the Nicene Church to consecrate a bishop with limited rights and limited powers. The chorepiscopoi, or bishops of rural areas, were always subordinate to a Metropolitan, and, as time went on, their authority was increasingly curtailed. But it was an entirely new thing for a bishop to retain only his title, and to have *all* his episcopal rights suspended. Any theologian of the time would have defined a bishop in terms of the functions he performed—presiding at the Liturgy, ordaining, etc. A bishop without functions would have seemed a contradiction in terms. Hence the punishment of Melitius was a remarkable one: the Fathers of Nicaea must have been very unwilling to grant him any status at all. To have granted him some semblance of episcopal status must have cost them a good deal. On the other hand, since the discrepancy between what they did and what they thought passed without comment, it is only too clear to us that they had no real understanding of the difference which ordination makes to a man. This is borne out by the regulations prescribed for the presbyters ordained by Melitius. Although we do not know exactly what the Nicene Fathers meant by *mystikotera cheirotonia*, it is obvious that they were not satisfied that Melitius' ordinations were quite valid. They were certain that they were irregular, but uncertain whether irregularity amounted to invalidity. And so, to be on the safe side, they prescribed a kind of re-ordination.

Similar rules were laid down for the reception of Nova-

[1] Hardouin. 1. 440E. Also Opitz. Bd. 1. 3. p. 48. 15.

tianist clergy in the Eighth Canon of Nicaea. Ex-Novatianist bishops were only to exercise episcopal functions in places where there were no Catholic clergy—otherwise they must be content with remaining presbyters or chorepiscopoi or whatever the Catholic Bishop thought fit for them to be, 'that there may not be two bishops in the city'. Admittedly this would lead to anomalies, but they would be resolved when the bishops concerned, whether Catholic or schismatic, died. Presbyters had to receive imposition of hands (*cheirothesia*) if they wished to be numbered amongst the clergy. The ambiguity of the terms *cheirothesia* and *mystikotera cheirotonia* gave rise to many discussions as to whether re-ordination or benediction was intended by the Nicene Fathers, but since C. H. Turner clinched the argument in favour of re-ordination, the matter has rested.[1]

If we re-open the discussion, it will not be out of dissatisfaction with C. H. Turner's judgment, but because we wish to approach the Nicene Fathers with a different question in mind. Turner asked them: 'By *cheirothesia*, did you mean a fresh ordination, or the use of the imposition of hands as a gesture of reconciliation?' We wish to ask them the question: 'When you decided on a fresh ordination, what purpose had you in mind? We have a problem which is similar to yours in one respect: we both are concerned with the resolution of a schism. But our schism is not of the same kind as yours, and in any case we should differ from you in that we should recognize the validity of Melitian and Novatianist orders. The point on which we want your guidance is this: Can the principles which guided you to a decision guide us also?'

Now the principles which guided the Nicene Fathers were undoubtedly these:

1. Before all other considerations must come the restoration of peace and unity to the Church. (If the Nicene Fathers had not felt this to be a theological necessity, they were forced to accept it as a political necessity by the Emperor, who had no patience with what he considered to be

---

[1] Essay on *Apostolic Succession* in *The Early History of the Church and the Ministry*. ed. H. B. Swete. p. 93. I owe much to this study of Patristic teaching.

hair-splitting differences of opinion on questions of Faith
and Order.)
2. Whatever form the reconciliation might take, it would
involve some re-adjustment of preconceived ideas about
the functions of a bishop and his status. For a time there
would have to be anomalies which would only be resolved when the present occupants of sees died.

Nowadays, although we are still guided by the same first
principle, we seem singularly reluctant to share the willing-
ness of the Nicene Fathers to accept the inevitability of a
temporary anomaly.

The practice of the Nicene Fathers was by no means
universal. The Church of Rome never took kindly to the
idea of re-ordination, and, as a general rule, refused to allow
penitent schismatics more than lay status, even if they had
been validly ordained. One of Novatian's consecrators, in
spite of his own valid consecration, was only accorded lay
status, after due penance, by Pope Cornelius.[1] In Milan,
however, when the Catholic Ambrose succeeded to the Arian
Auxentius, he treated the Arian clergy as valid ministers of
the sacraments, for the sake of the peace of the Church.
'Ambrose . . . received those who had received ordination
from Auxentius . . . and they received many others in the
East who had not been ordained by the orthodox, lest, if
these remained outside, the heresy of the Arians should
strike root, and the flocks perish, and the greater portion of
the body of the nations be lost. In this way they treated both
those of Palestine and Phoenice and many others; properly
relaxing the strict rules of ordination for the sake of the
salvation of the nations' (Theophilus of Alexandria).[2]

What Theophilus of Alexandria calls a 'proper relaxation
of strict rules' came to be known as *economy*. We may define
it as the *adaptation of a means to an end*. It does not mean that
the worthiness of an end justifies any means of achieving it;
neither does it mean that a single bishop was justified in
adapting generally accepted rules to achieve an end in his

[1] Corn. Papa. ap. Eus. *h.e.* 6. 43. 10.
[2] cit. ap. Severus of Antioch. ed. E. W. Brooks. op. cit. Vol. 2, Part 2, p. 304.

own particular diocese. It means that a Council or a bishop, acting in consultation with other bishops, may modify generally recognized rules of Church Order to secure no less an end than the salvation of the nations. Athanasius declared that Catholic clergy who had been unwillingly or forcibly involved in schism might be pardoned and reinstated by the exercise of *economy*.[1] Basil the Great wrote in his Canonical letter to Amphilochius that certain bishops in Asia had agreed to accept schismatical Baptism as valid, *for the sake of economy*.[2]

Nowadays, the Principle of Economy is spoken of, as though it were an established doctrine which enables certain modifications to be made in the accepted rules of Church Order.[3] I do not think that the Fathers ever thought of economy in this way. It was their custom to consider what action it was necessary to take in any particular case of schism, in the interests of charity and good government. They then proceeded to take action, and, if it were necessary to modify or adapt the rules of Church Order, to say that they had done so *economically*. They always dealt with the facts of a case, and did what was necessary to remove obstacles to the unity of the Church; they never defined a doctrine of economy, or used any such notion as a guide. Hence they would seem to advise us to deal with our difficulties in a way that the Holy Spirit shows us the situation demands, and then to admit that we have acted economically. They would not commend us to think how far 'economy' permits us to stretch a means, in order to achieve an end.

The worst of the Eastern schisms, the Meletian Schism of Antioch,[4] was an extremely complicated affair which lasted

---

[1] *Ep. Rufin.* (PG. 26. 1180C). N.B. Athanasius refused to reinstate those who had initiated schism.

[2] *Ep.* 188. 1 (PG. 32. 669A).

[3] The Bishops assembled at Lambeth in 1930 came near to this error: they held that if the Anglican Church were to be in communion with the C.S.I., while the C.S.I. was in communion with other non-episcopal churches, an anomalous situation would arise which would be covered by the Principle of Economy. They defined *economy* as 'administrative action to meet a temporary situation without prejudice to any principle of ecclesiastical order'. Report of the Lambeth Conference 1930. Ch. 3. Part 1. *The Unity of the Church.* p. 123.

[4] Not to be confused with the Melitian schism of Egypt, vid. sup. p. 50.

for over half a century (A.D. 362–414). At one time there were four Bishops of Antioch, of whom we are concerned with two: Meletius, recognized as orthodox by the East, and Paulinus, recognized by the West. Neither Bishop could claim to have been regularly consecrated: Meletius was tarred with the Arian brush, and Paulinus had been irregularly consecrated in A.D. 362 by Lucifer of Cagliari.[1] Moreover, in defiance of the 23rd Canon of the Council of Antioch, Paulinus consecrated Evagrius to succeed him. Nevertheless the Roman Pope continued to recognize Paulinus and his successors, in spite of the irregularity of their consecration, while the Easterns continued to recognize the successors of Meletius, in spite of his Arian tendencies.[2]

The schism is not of great theological interest to us to-day, but is does show us how schisms are prolonged. The Antiochene Schism need not have lasted half so long, if;

1. Both parties had agreed to have the authenticity and regularity of their orders independently examined; and
2. Both parties had put first the need for united witness to Faith in Our Lord Jesus Christ.

As regards 1, it may be mentioned, in passing, that an independent Roman Catholic theologian, who has made a study of the C.S.I., is of the opinion that the Church of England ought to recognize the validity of the orders of the C.S.I. As regards 2, the harm done at Antioch by a fifty-year schism ought to make us chary of waiting for fifty years until we determine what the relationship between the Church of England and the C.S.I. is to be.

So far, we have discussed only the schisms of the Eastern half of Christendom, and the methods which the Eastern Fathers adopted to deal with them. But when the Eastern, John Chrysostom, said that schism was no less an evil than heresy,[3] he spoke for all the Doctors of the Church. East and West agreed that whereas a heresiarch was creating some-

---

[1] He acted alone and without a mandate. Paulinus' error consisted in consecrating his successor during his tenure of the see.

[2] Chrysostom, in fact, unchurched the adherents of Evagrius, cf. *Hom.* 11. 5 *in Eph.* (Gaume. 11. 87A).

[3] *hom.* 11. 5 *in Eph.* (Gaume. 11. 88A).

thing that was essentially not a church but a sect, a schismatic was attacking the unity of the Body of Christ more directly. He therefore was guilty of as grave a sin as heresy, if not graver, because, being orthodox in faith, he ought to know better than to confound the order of the Church. That is why the Fathers clung to the rule that there must never be two bishops in one place.[2] The bishop represented the unity of the Church. When he spoke, he spoke with the authority of Christ. When he celebrated the Holy Mysteries, he celebrated them by the authority of Christ on behalf of the whole company of the faithful committed to his charge. To have two bishops in one place made havoc of that simple unity. Two people cannot exercise one authority; two people cannot represent the unity of a worshipping congregation.

And so, when the Western Fathers had to deal with the Novatianist schism after the Decian persecution, their first thought was naturally to unchurch the schismatics, and cut them off altogether from communion with the members of the One Body of Christ. By this time, however, they had learned that too severe a discipline did not succeed in correcting grave sins—it only made schisms more bitter. Consequently, whilst they continued to regard the sin of schism with as much loathing as the sin of heresy, they were usually prepared to treat offenders more leniently than they would have done at the beginning of the Third Century.

The change of heart, however, brought them into a fresh dilemma, because both Novatian and Donatus went into schism on this very question of lenience. They were both men of puritanical temperament, who considered that no punishment could be severe enough for lapsed Christians. They held that to admit them to communion even after public penance was a betrayal of Christian principles; a bishop who treated the lapsed with such magnanimity was not worthy of his place. Therefore they refused to regard him as a Catholic Bishop, and set themselves up as the Bishops of the Catholic Church instead.

In Africa, then, after the Decian and Diocletianic persecutions, there were two rival claimants to most of the sees,

[2] *C. Nic.* (325). *can.* 8.

each with their own churches and congregations. The Catholic Bishops' claim to orthodoxy rested on their succession in office from the first bishops,[1] whilst the schismatical bishops' claim rested on what they felt was a more Catholic and Apostolic administration of Christian discipline. But the problem was infinitely more complex than that. In the main, the African temperament seems to have leaned more towards the side of rigorism than towards the side of lenience. Montanism and Novatianism both became more strongly rooted in Africa than elsewhere, simply because they were based on rigorist interpretations of the Gospel. Thus, with a few exceptions, the schismatical bishops were abler men by far than the Catholic, and the reconciliation of schismatics in that country was far more difficult than in Syria or Egypt. Moreover, whilst Cyprian had been moderately lenient in his treatment of the lapsed, he had been a rigorist in so far as he had steadfastly refused to recognize the validity of sacraments celebrated by them. The Donatists therefore, at a later date, claimed the support of the Catholic Cyprian in this respect, and Augustine had to re-interpret Cyprian to them in his treatise *De Baptismo*, almost to the extent of re-writing what Cyprian had said.

Cyprian's vision of the Unity of the Church was clearer than that of any of the Doctors of the Church since St. Paul. 'There is one Body and one Spirit, even as ye are called in one hope of your calling, One Lord, One Faith, One Baptism, One God' (Eph. iv. 4)[2]—this is the keynote of all that he wrote. The Holy Spirit, being One and Undivided, acts only within the One and Undivided Church—He cannot be present with those who have seceded from it.[3] Cyprian therefore refused to recognize the validity of the orders of any minister outside the Church, even if he had at one time been ordained within the Church.[4] No sacrament could have any

[1] Optatus. 2. 3, 4. (PL. 11. 948 ff.)
[2] cf. *De Unitate*. 4, 5. (CSEL. pp. 212 ff). On this section see S. L. Greenslade. *Schism in the Early Church*, p. 168. I am greatly indebted to Dr. Greenslade for the help I have received from this book.
[3] *Ep.* 74. 4.
[4] He refused to acknowledge Basilides as Bishop of Leon-Astorga, because he had compromised with the secular authorities during the persecution and had obtained a certificate of sacrifice. This in spite of the reinstatement of Basilides in his see by Pope Stephen. *Ep.* 67.

validity or efficacy apart from the Church in which Christ intended it to be celebrated: any minister who seceded from the Church *ipso facto* lost irrevocably the gift of the Spirit which had validated his orders.

Cyprian's view of Novatian's schism was consequently straightforward and consistent. First, Novatian had procured his own consecration at a time when Cornelius had already been consecrated Bishop of Rome—*ergo* his episcopal orders were null and void.[1] But even if he had been properly consecrated, he could not have retained his episcopal status, because he had fallen away from the unity of his fellow-bishops.[2] Secondly, no sacraments celebrated by the Novatianists had any validity, even though they used the same formulae of administration as the Catholic Church. 'For when (at Baptism) they say "Dost thou believe in the remission of sins and in eternal life through the Holy Church?" they lie in their interrogatory, since they have no Church. Then moreover they themselves confess with their own mouths that remission of sins can only be given by the Holy Church; and, not having this, they show that sins cannot be remitted with them.'[3]

Cyprian's policy when dealing with schismatics was:

1. To re-baptize all who had received schismatical baptism; and
2. To admit to lay communion only, after penance, all clerics who had seceded and wished to return.

On the second point he had already crossed swords with the Pope of Rome;[4] a much more vehement controversy arose between him and Stephen on the question of re-baptism. Stephen, following the custom of his see, recognized schismatical baptism if the correct formula had been used; his practice was to admit those who had been baptized in schism to communion after imposition of hands. 'But what is the point of laying hands on them?' asks Cyprian. 'If you believe that schismatics have the power to administer valid

---

[1] *Ep.* 44.

[2] *Ep.* 55. 24. (CSEL. p. 643. 3). episcopatum autem tenere non posset, etiam si episcopus prius factus a coepiscoporum suorum corpore et ab ecclesiae unitate descisceret.

[3] *Ep.* 69. 7.   [4] vid. sup. p. 57. n. 4.

baptism, why should you not allow the validity of their laying-on of hands also?'[1] He scorns Stephen's appeal to the tradition of the Church of Rome, and asks ironically where the basis for it is to be found in the New Testament.[2] Better to acknowledge the tradition wrong, he says, than to perpetuate an error; those who had already been admitted to communion without re-baptism should be commended to the Lord's mercy.[3]

Cyprian was not alone in the Baptism controversy with Stephen; he had the written support of Firmilian of Caesaraea,[4] and the oral support of 87 Bishops in Council at Carthage (A.D. 256). Cyril of Jerusalem also re-baptized heretics,[5] and Athanasius re-baptized Arians, on the grounds that Arians did not mean what the Church meant when they baptized in the threefold Name.[6] In the main, the Easterns sided with Cyprian rather than with Stephen, with the exception of Dionysius of Alexandria, who seems to have been a law to himself, adopting a policy midway between those of Stephen and Cyprian.[7] If an oecumenical vote had been taken in A.D. 256, there is little doubt that Cyprian's practice would have been universally adopted by a majority decision. Fortunately the first Oecumenical Council was 70 years ahead, and it actually adopted Stephen's practice, previously made the rule for the Western Church at the Council of Arles in A.D. 314.[8]

An anonymous treatise, *De Rebaptismate*,[9] written in Africa at the time of Cyprian's controversy with Stephen, suggests some of the difficulties in accepting Cyprian's views, which eventually led to the reversal of his policy. First, the invocation of the Trinity in Baptism must always have some efficacy, whether inside or outside the Church. The Lord

[1] (Cyprian made no real distinction between the gift of the Spirit conferred at Confirmation, and the gift conferred on penitents). *Ep*. 74. 5, paraphrased.
[2] *Ep*. 74. 2.
[3] *Ep*. 73. 23.
[4] *Ep*. ap. *Epp*. Cyp. 75. (CSEL. p. 810).
[5] *Procat*. 7. (PG. 33. 345B).
[6] *Or. c. Ar*. 2. 42 (PG. 26. 237 A, B).
[7] See Lawlor and Oulton, Eusebius. *h.e.* Vol. 2. pp. 240 ff. Also Feltoe. *Dionysius of Alexandria*. CPT. pp. 40 ff.
[8] *can*. 8.
[9] Printed in the Appendix to Cyprian's Works. CSEL. 3. 3. p. 69.

would not have referred to those enemies of His who pro-
phesied and cast out devils in His Name, if the invocation
of His Name, *per se*, was inefficacious.[1] Secondly, if schismatics are unworthy ministers of Baptism, what about
bishops with immoral characters who yet remain in the
Church? And what about orthodox bishops who are none
too accurate and precise about the formulae of administration? Where is the line to be drawn between an unworthy
and a worthy minister?[2]

A hundred years later, Optatus of Milev took these sugges-
tions a stage further in his anti-Donatist treatise. Like
Cyprian he makes the unity of the Church the foundation of
his argument—'The Church is One and its unity is derived
from its sacraments.[3] But, unlike Cyprian, he maintains that
the unworthiness of the minister makes no difference to the
validity or sanctity of the sacraments of the Church—
'Sacraments are holy in themselves, and not through men'.[4]
He had come to realize that the Donatist Schism, more for-
midable by far than the Novatianist, could not be classed as
a sect. Its members must have received something of the
Grace of God at their Baptism; furthermore, if the schism
were ever to be resolved, the Catholic Church would have to
make an open recognition of the fact. But he failed to make
his own views clear, and never actually says what he thought
the effect of schismatical baptism was.

Augustine of Hippo continued the discussion some 50
years later. He insists that there is no such thing as a 'schismatical' or 'heretical' baptism—baptism is always the Baptism of Christ into His Church.[5] A man who is baptized in
schism is truly baptized, *but* on account of the sinfulness of
his separation from the peace and charity of the Church, he
does not receive the benefit of his baptism until he is incorporated into the Body of Christ.[6] It is the same with regard

---

[1] 7. p. 78.
[2] 10. p. 81.
[3] Ecclesia una est cuius sanctitas de sacramentis colligitur. 2. 1. (PL. 11.
941A).
[4] Sacramenta per se esse sancta, non per homines. 5. 4. (PL. 11. 1053A).
[5] Non est baptismus ille schismaticorum vel haereticorum, sed dei et
ecclesiae. *De Baptismo*. 1. 14 (22). (CSEL. 51. p. 166. 12).
[6] *Bapt.* 1. 13 (21). p. 165. 26.

to ordination—a bishop consecrated in schism is truly a bishop, but his orders are not of use or benefit to him whilst he remains in schism. Not until he is received into the Catholic Church (without re-ordination) are his orders efficacious.[1]

It is commonly believed that Augustine closed the discussion in the Early Church, and that his definition that sacraments celebrated outside the Church are valid but not efficacious was generally accepted. This is not so—the Second Council of Saragossa in A.D. 592,[2] and the First Council of Orleans in A.D. 511,[3] both required the re-ordination of Arian clergy who desired to hold clerical office in the Catholic Church. Moreover, where the Catholic Church has allowed schismatical baptism to be valid, it has usually allowed it to be in some degree efficacious. The truth is that validity and efficacy are in practice inseparable: converts to Christianity, baptized in schism, become different men, just as those who receive Catholic Baptism—the sacrament has some effect on them. Clergymen in schismatical churches undoubtedly exercise an effective ministry, even though it is not the same ministry as that of clergymen in the Catholic Church. Consequently, Augustine's definition has, during the last millenium, been turned inside out. We now allow some efficacy to schismatical orders, but question their validity.

How then shall we apply the teaching of the Western Fathers to our present situation? The advice they would give us would be, I think, something like this:

1. Put first things first. Ask yourselves how the schisms with which you are confronted stand vis-à-vis the One Holy Catholic Church. Then ask yourselves how you stand vis-à-vis the Church. It is no use putting all your confidence in the security of your own position within the tactual line of Apostolic Succession, if you are uncertain whether the sin of schism may not have damaged your own Catholicity.

2. Begin discussing the sacraments at the beginning. Do not discuss the Sacrament of Holy Orders until you have answered the question: 'What is our relationship in the

---

[1] ep. Parm. 2. 13 (28). p. 79. 3.
[2] Canon 11.　　　[3] Canon 10.

61

Body of Christ to those who have received the same baptism, but are not in the same communion?'

3. The argument about the distinction between validity and efficacy has turned full circle, and you are no wiser now than when we began it. Think in your own language, not ours. You do not think of Grace in the same language as we did; you think of it as the very influence of Christ Himself. Get out of the way of thinking about Holy Orders as mechanically as we thought about Grace. Think out how Christ influences the men whom he calls to be His ministers in the C.S.I.

When we read the early history of the Church and its ministry, we see two things clearly. First: The Church gradually moves into the present custom of episcopal consecration; not because it is of the *esse* of the Church—if it had been, the first-century church would have been no Church, and the third-century Church of Alexandria would have been no Church; not because it is of the *bene esse* of the Church—if it had been, Aerius, who held that episcopal and presbyteral orders were identical, would not have been condemned;[1] but because it is a mark of the fullness and the wholeness of the Body of Christ.

Secondly, we see the Church wounded and divided by long and bitter schisms. It is the glory of the Fathers, whom we have consulted, that it was their first aim to heal and to restore—that they saw everything they did, not against the background of some minor anomaly in their own local churches, but against the background of the Salvation of the Nations.

---

[1] A.D. 355. See Epiph. *haer.* 75. 4 (GCS. p. 336. 11; PG. 42. 509A).

IV

EPISCOPACY IN THE WORKS OF THE ELIZABETHAN AND CAROLINE DIVINES

B. D. Till

I am very well persuaded that the see of Rome will never hear of any terms of reconcilement, so long as they see our divisions increase. But I am very well assured, that the divisions of the Reformation can never be reunited, so as to prevent the like for the future; but upon that ground, which, being received, will serve to reunite the whole Church.

HERBERT THORNDIKE: 'Of the Forbearance or Penalties which a due Reformation requires.'[1]

'WE do not arrogate to ourselves either a new Church, or a new religion or new Holy Orders. . . . Our religion is the same it was, our Church the same it was, our Holy Orders the same they were, in substance; differing only from what they were formerly, as a garden weeded from a garden unweeded.'[2] Archbishop Bramhall used these striking words in 1654 to describe the Church of England, catholic and reformed. Nearly a century earlier John Jewel, the first Anglican apologist, was in effect saying the same when he wrote, 'We succeed the bishops that have been before our days, we are elected, consecrate, confirmed, and admitted, as they were.'[3] The century was one of many vicissitudes, political and religious, for the *Ecclesia Anglicana*; at the outset of the Elizabethan settlement it was on the one hand threatened by the forces of Rome, till lately established at home and seemingly until the Armada still dominant abroad, and on

---

[1] H. Thorndike, *Works*, vol. V, p. 404. (Library of Anglo-Catholic Theology, Oxford, 1851.)

[2] J. Bramhall *Works*, (L.A.C.T.), vol. I, p. 199. (*A Just Vindication of the Church of England*.)

[3] J. Jewel, 'The Defence of the Apology of the Church of England', II, v. I. (*Works*, Parker Society, Cambridge, 1848.)

the other subject to the thorough-going attacks of the Genevan reformers, who were within an ace of capturing Parliament in 1572 while at about the same time making substantial inroads into the organization of the Church. There followed a period of comparative peace, from the closing decade of the reign of Elizabeth and through that of James I, until the ill-advised attempts of Charles I to force the Prayer Book on Scotland brought affairs both political and religious to a crisis; this was a period of consolidation and it is adorned by the work in their various spheres of Hooker, of Andrewes and of Laud. But the century ends with the Church in exile, caught and nearly crushed between the Roman and Genevan millstones, yet stating more valiantly than ever the principles of the *via media* for which it stood. It is the purpose of this essay to show how these principles, especially where they centred on the vital issue of episcopacy, were at first seen tentatively then expounded more fully, but always with a striking continuity, by the representative divines of the first century of Anglican history.

It fell to John Jewel, Bishop of Salisbury, to lay the foundations. He produced his *Apologia pro Ecclesia Anglicana* in 1562, and the longer and more polemically vigorous *Defence* in 1570, by which time Elizabeth was prepared to feel a little less non-committal towards the Roman opponents of her religious settlement. Jewel had been an exile under the Marian regime and was a definite Protestant, but not of the Genevan persuasion. When he speaks of the reformers it is nearly always Luther and Zwingli, rather than Calvin, of whom he is thinking, and his theological speculation, where he permits himself that luxury, may be said to be Lutheran in emphasis. His work must not be discounted as that of a Protestant extremist; he must rather be thought of as a typical Anglican churchman of the period. If he had not been that he would hardly have been chosen, in those anxious early days of the settlement, as the official Anglican apologist. Such was his position not only for the Elizabethan but also for the Caroline divines, as can be seen in a significant passage where Bramhall, defending the Anglican retention of episcopacy, cites as his authorities the Prayer Book, the Ordinal, the Articles and, in the same breath, Jewel's Apology.[1]

Thus all through his book the voice of the Church of England can be recognized providing the harmonies to the burden of the Protestant tune. The Protestant in him sets up the word of God as the test of the catholicity of the church, and the orthodoxy of its members, but the Anglican in him says 'in this conference and judgement of the Holy Scriptures we need oftentimes the discretion and wisdom of learned fathers', thus establishing, in striking contrast to the Genevan insistence on the unadorned word of God, the appeal of the *Ecclesia Anglicana* to the primitive and undivided church.[2] 'We for our part, have learned of Christ, of the Apostles, of the devout fathers', he affirms, and clinches the argument, 'verily in the judgement of the godly five hundred of those first years are worth more than the whole thousand years that followed afterward.'[3] He knows that the Church of England is being accused of schism and, realizing the gravity of the charge,[4] in common with many Anglican apologists who followed him, he takes it hardly. But the blame for schism must be laid at the door of the Pope who 'to feed his ambition and greediness of rule hath . . . rent whole Christendom asunder'.[5] The Church of England has been forced to return to the higher (i.e. the more primitive) ground where the wells have not run dry; she must therefore be acquitted of the charge of schism for 'he seemeth not to depart from the church, that bodily departeth; but he that spiritually leaveth the foundations of the ecclesiastical truth. . . . We are departed forth from them in the sight of man; they are departed from us in the judgement of God.'[6] 'We have indeed put ourselves apart, not, as heretics are wont, from the Church of Christ . . . but from the infection of naughty

---

[1] Bramhall, *Works*, vol. III, pp. 471–2. Hooker's opinion of Jewel was that he was 'the worthiest divine that Christendom hath bred for the space of some hundreds of years'. *Ecclesiastical Polity*, II, vi, 4.

[2] Jewel, *Defence* IV, xviii, I & I, ix, I. Jewel confesses to a particular predilection, among the Fathers, for Augustine, Jerome and Ambrose.

[3] ibid., *Apology* III, i, I and *Defence* I, iv, 3.

[4] ibid, *Apology* V, i, I, and IV, ix, 2. 'It is doubtless an odious matter for one to leave the fellowship whereunto he hath been accustomed.'

[5] ibid. VI, i, 3.

[6] ibid., *Defence* V, xii, 2.

persons and hypocrites . . . and to say truly we do not despise the church of these men . . . partly for the name's sake itself, and partly for that the gospel of Jesus Christ hath once been therein truly and purely set forth.'[1] This was, of course, to show surprising moderation for those days; such sentiments foreshadow the determination of Hooker to preserve the best of the catholic heritage in and for the Church of England. Elsewhere, for instance, Jewel, while repudiating the Pope's claims to the absolute and unique right of succeeding St. Peter—'lawful succession standeth not only in possession of place, but also, and much rather, in doctrine and diligence' —yet is not unwilling to 'grant somewhat to succession'.[2] He does not go so far as explicitly to vest succession in the episcopate, but points out that the powers arrogated to the Mediaeval papacy are those which should properly belong to the episcopate, asking, if through papal infallibility 'there can no harm come to the church, what need is there to retain to no purpose the names of bishops? . . . The names only they bear and do nothing. For, if there be no sheep that may stray, why be they called shepherds?'[3] In face of these papal claims he asserts firmly the Anglican view of the Cyprianic episcopate: 'as many baptisms are but one baptism; even so saith St. Cyprian, many bishoprics are but one bishopric, and therein as well the bishop of Rome as also every other several bishop hath his portion. I say the bishoprick of Rome is not this whole bishoprick but a part, not the body of the sun, but a beam.'[4] Beyond this, and the plain statement that 'we believe there be divers degrees of ministers in the church; whereof some be deacons, some priests, some bishops',[5] he is not prepared to go. There is no attempt either to define the function or to trace the history of episcopacy.

Another Elizabethan defender of the religious settlement was John Whitgift, who in 1583 succeeded the lax but heroic Grindal as Archbishop of Canterbury, and than whom, in the words of Professor Norman Sykes 'the Elizabethan church

[1] ibid., *Apology* IV, ix, 2.
[2] ibid., *Defence* I, v, 4 and *Apology* VI, xxi, 1.
[3] ibid., *Apology* IV, xii, 1.
[4] ibid., *Defence* II, iii, 5.
[5] ibid., *Apology* II, iii, 1.

had no harder *malleus Puritanorum*'.[1] Among his activities in this capacity were his replies to the first and second 'Admonition to Parliament', the high-water mark of the Presbyterian bid to capture the Church through the machinery of the state. Starting from the then traditional Protestant and Anglican[2] definition that 'the essential notes of the church be these only: the true preaching of the word of God, and the right administration of the sacraments', he vigorously attacks the Presbyterians for their 'very popish conclusion' in making the matter of government an essential mark of the church. Some sort of government is of course necessary for the church in the world, 'but that any one kind of government is so necessary that without it the church cannot be saved, or that it may not be altered into some other kind thought to be more expedient, I utterly deny.'[3] He goes on to draw an interesting distinction between the perfection and the essence of a church: 'government, or some kind of government, may be a part of the church, touching the outward form or perfection of it, yet it is not such a part of the essence and being, but that it may be the church of Christ without this or that kind of government; and therefore "the kind of government" of the church is not "necessary unto salvation"!'[4] We shall find this distinction being repeated with growing emphasis in the seventeenth century.

Here then, in Jewel and Whitgift, are the opinions of two of the leading prelates of the Elizabethan church, faced with

---

[1] Norman Sykes, *The Church of England and Non-episcopal Churches in the Sixteenth and Seventeenth Centuries*, p. 11. The publication of this pamphlet was followed by a lively exchange of letters between Professor Sykes on the one hand and Mr. Eric Kemp and the late Dom Gregory Dix on the other. (*Theology* 1949.) The point at issue was whether there could be said to be, as Dr. Sykes claimed, an 'Anglican tradition' in the seventeenth century. It seems to the present writer that the Dixie Professor fully maintained his case that the writers he had cited in his pamphlet (who are by and large those quoted in this essay, i.e. Hooker, Andrewes, Taylor, Cosin, Bramhall and Thorndike), not only form a recognisable body of opinion, but also may be said to be 'representative Caroline high-churchmen', at least as far as the first half of the century is concerned. They are the weightiest names among the Anglicans then writing, and it was in the main they whom the Tractarians chose to have reprinted under the *aegis* of the Library of Anglo-Catholic Theology.

[2] Article XIX.

[3] J. Whitgift, *The Defence of the Answer to the Admonition*, Works (Parker Society, 1851), vol. I, pp. 182, 184.

[4] ibid., p. 185.

the unenviable task of working out the peculiar Anglican settlement. They were armed with the Ordinal and its preface along with the Articles, which taken together 'it is legitimate to interpret . . . as affirming the resolve of the Church of England to continue the traditional historical threefold ministry and to maintain episcopal ordination and government'.[1] But they did not attempt to erect on these foundations any speculative theology of the episcopate in its relation to the being of the church. The weight of the evidence militates against the claim that 'the official attitude of the (Elizabethan) Church emphatically was . . . that the bishops and the bishops alone . . . constitute in themselves that essential body of persons without which there could be no Church.'[2] The Elizabethan bishops continued the episcopal government of the church in its traditional methods and function, not so much because of any theory of episcopacy, as because this was the custom of the Church *in* England, which, in their belief and through their actions, remained the Church *of* England.

It is not, however, the ruthless John Whitgift, but rather the gentle and judicious Richard Hooker who is remembered as the theological advocate of the *Ecclesia Anglicana* against the Presbyterianizing party who, in his own words, 'require in us the utter relinquishment of all things Popish . . . government or ceremonies or whatsoever it be.'[3] The largeness of his mind, not to say the wonder of his prose, raised this great Englishman above the dust of controversy, and in the world which his genius created there were laid the foundations of a *rationale* of Anglicanism, which the Church of England neglects to its peril. It was Hooker who rescued and preserved for us the best of the mediaeval philosophical heritage, the twin beliefs in human wisdom and the divine law. He saw the danger of the anti-rational tendency in Puritan thought: 'to infringe the force and strength of man's testimony were to shake the very fortress of God's truth.'[4] He saw too that in making 'the name and light of nature an unlucky comet . . .

---

[1] Sykes, *op cit*, p. 7.
[2] *The Apostolic Ministry* (ed. K. E. Kirk), p. 406.
[3] Richard Hooker, *Of the Laws of Ecclesiastical Polity*, IV, iii, 1.
[4] ibid., II, vii, 3.

as if God had so accursed it, that it should never shine or give light in things concerning our duty any way towards him', the Puritans not only struck at 'the estimation and credit of man', but also threatened 'to overthrow such laws and constitutions in the Church as . . . if they should be taken away, would peradventure leave neither face nor memory of Church to continue long in the world.'[1] Against this anti-rationalism, he claims that reason is the 'framer and perceiver of laws' both for the state and the Church, those of the latter being framed in general councils, which were apostolic in origin.[2] It is tempting, he admits, because it would make better material for his anti-Puritan arguments, to say that all religious matters, including the question of church government, can be found immutably instituted in scripture; but this is not so.[3] On the contrary, positive laws (i.e. all other than natural laws), even those instituted by God, are mutable and only continue to be binding as long as they fulfil the object for which they were first created; if they fail to do this, or if that object ceases to exist, then the laws can be changed or cancelled. As an example Hooker gives the Jewish laws which, even though God-given, may under the new dispensation be abrogated by men.[4] The laws for church government fall within this mutable category, and of their alteration the Church is the arbiter: 'I therefore conclude, that neither God's being author of laws for government of His Church, nor his committing them unto Scripture, is any reason sufficient wherefore all churches should for ever be bound to keep them without change. . . .Touching things which belong to discipline and outward polity, the Church hath authority to make canons, laws and decrees, even as we read that in the Apostles' time it did.'[5] 'Discipline and outward polity' are matters which for Hooker explicitly include the ordering of the Church's ministry. For him the Church holds the central, determinative and legislative, position in ecclesiastical polity. No statement could be more

[1] ibid., IV, viii, 4 and II, vii, 1.
[2] ibid., I, x, *passim*.
[3] ibid., III, x, 8.
[4] ibid., I, xv, I and I, xv, 3.
[5] ibid., III, x, 7.

definite than those cited above, to the effect that it is the Church which makes and controls its ministry, rather than that the ministry gives being to the Church. His doctrine of episcopacy, stated in Book VII, is high, but his doctrine of the Church, here expounded, is higher.[1]

In Book VII Hooker defines the office of a bishop by stating his powers: he has 'a power to be by way of jurisdiction a pastor even to pastors themselves'; the things 'which do properly make him a bishop, cannot be common unto him with other pastors', his superiority to them lying both in the latitude and jurisdiction of his power; presbyters' powers are but lights borrowed from the episcopal lamp.[2] He is not afraid to be 'bold and peremptory' in saying that, 'if anything in the Church's government, surely the first institution of bishops was from heaven, was even of God'.[3] He bases this claim on the fact that 'the first bishops in the Church were his blessed Apostles' and that from their days 'a thousand five hundred years and upward the Church of Christ hath now continued under the sacred regiment of bishops. Neither for so long hath Christianity been ever planted in any kingdom throughout the world but with this kind of government alone.'[4] He himself inclines to the view that historically the institution of the office preceded its title, and can therefore be pushed back to the earliest days of the Church, even to the persons of the Apostles themselves, who, as eyewitnesses of the Incarnation have no successors, but as holders of jurisdiction still find their 'true successors' in the bishops.[5] Yet for all that, remembering the principles he has stated, he maintains that the bishops 'albeit they may

[1] It is a fact that seeming discrepancies between the earlier books, in which Hooker lays down his principles, and the later, in which he applies them, have caused some doubt to be thrown on the authenticity of these later books. Certainly in Book VII he seems to put forward a more 'advanced' doctrine of episcopacy than that which might have been expected by the reader of the first four books. Nevertheless he says nothing which specifically contradicts the fundamentals there expounded; in these earlier books he postulates a doctrine of the authority of the Church high enough to 'contain' the view of episcopacy later advanced. It will suffice then, for our present purposes, to allow the authenticity of Book VII.

[2] ibid., VII, ii, 3 and VII, vi, *passim*.
[3] ibid., VII, v, 10.
[4] ibid., VII, iv, 1 and VII, i, 4.
[5] ibid., VII, iv, 4.

avouch with conformity of truth that their authority hath thus descended even from the very apostles themselves, yet the absolute and everlasting continuance of it they cannot say that any commandment of the Lord doth enjoin; and therefore must acknowledge that the Church hath power by universal consent upon urgent cause to take it away, if thereunto she be constrained.'[1] On the other hand even if we allow, as is possible, that the office grew up after the death of the apostles, 'this order taken by the Church itself (for so let us suppose that the Apostles did neither by word or deed appoint it) were notwithstanding more warrantable than that it should give place and be abrogated, because the ministry of the Gospel and the functions thereof ought to be from heaven.'[2] So in either case, whether the episcopate is apostolic in origin or not, Hooker makes his point that it is subject to the over-riding legislative power of the Church.

Hooker recognized the existence both of the problem of intercommunion, and of an intransigent approach to that problem: 'Now whereas some do infer, that no ordination can stand but only such as is made by bishops, which have had their ordination likewise by other bishops before them, till we come to the very Apostles of Christ themselves . . . to this we answer that there may be sometimes very just and sufficient reason to allow ordination made without a bishop. The whole Church visible being the true original subject of all power, it hath not ordinarily allowed any other than bishops alone to ordain: howbeit, as the ordinary course is ordinarily in all things to be observed, so it may be in some cases not unnecessary that we decline from the ordinary ways.' These cases he procedes to enumerate: 'Men may be extraordinarily, yet allowably, two ways admitted unto spiritual functions in the Church. One is, when God himself doth of himself raise up any, whose labour he useth without requiring that men should authorize them; but then he doth ratify their calling by manifest signs and tokens himself from heaven. . . . Another extraordinary kind of vocation is, when the exigence of necessity doth constrain to leave the usual ways of the Church,

---

[1] ibid., VII, v, 8.
[2] ibid., VII, xi, 8.

which otherwise we would willingly keep; where the Church
must needs have some ordained, and neither hath nor can
have possibly a bishop to ordain; in case of such necessity
the ordinary institution of God hath given oftentimes, and
may give, place. And therefore we are not simply without
exception to urge a lineal descent of power from the Apostles
by continued succession of bishops in every effectual ordination. These cases of inevitable necessity excepted, none may
ordain but only bishops; by the imposition of their hands it
is, that the Church giveth power of order, both unto presbyters and deacons.'[1] The first of his exceptions might be
said to apply to-day to those free church ministries which
have been manifest recipients of the grace of God; the second
was held in Hooker's day to apply to the ministries of the
Continental Reformed Churches.

The first four books *Of the Laws of the Ecclesiastical Polity*
appeared in 1594. By then the Church of England had suc-
cessfully defended the position established in the Elizabethan
Settlement, and the attacks on that position both from Rome
and Geneva had spent their original force. For nearly half
a century it was allowed a period of respite in which, through
the thought of Hooker and those who followed him, the
influence of Andrewes and other saintly pastors, and the
reforms of Laud and his party, it produced a distinctive
ethos of its own. Yet the *Ecclesia Anglicana* could not afford to
be insular; for there was no escaping the fact that religiously
(and more often than not politically) the established church
at home and the reformed churches abroad were allied
against the rising power of the Counter Reformation. Anglicans were therefore aware that they could not ignore the
question of orders, a question on which the Protestant
churches abroad held and maintained a position which was
unmistakably alien to that of the Church of England. This
problem was posed in its most acute and practical form
when, the period of respite having ended with disaster for
the Church of England, a handful of her exiles found themselves during the Commonwealth living cheek by jowl with
Roman Catholics and Calvinists in France and the Low

[1] ibid., VII, xiv, 11.

Countries. One, at least, of them cut the Gordian knot. It was the experience of the catholic-minded John Cosin that whereas the Roman Catholics 'excommunicate us, and abhor to join with us in any sacred action either of prayer or sacraments . . . the Reformed Churches do most willingly receive us into their churches, and frequently repair to ours, joining with us both in prayers and sacraments.'[1] This experience led him to overcome his scruples and to communicate with the French Huguenots at Charenton.

It is, however, with the thought of the Anglican divines, rather than with their practice, that this essay is mainly concerned.[2] With Hooker there emerges a theology which is neither Roman nor Genevan, but recognisably Anglican, catholic and reformed. In the course of the seventeenth century this theology was to develop very much along the lines sketched out by him; especially where it deals with the vexed question of episcopacy, the thought of the Carolines bears the marks of the influence of Hooker. Not, of course, that they were all of one mind on this question which so soon was seen to be the focus of more than one problem. Richard Montague, for instance, 'held an exclusive doctrine of the episcopacy by which the reformed churches of the Continent were unchurched. His principle, succinctly stated, was: "non est sacerdotium nisi in ecclesia, non est ecclesia sine sacerdotio".'[3] But Montague was a rare, if not an unique, bird. There was a more numerous and influential party which took precisely the opposite view and regarded the question of order as of secondary importance. This party included men like Williams, Bishop of Lincoln, Lord Keeper

---

[1] John Cosin, *Works* (L.A.C.T.), vol. IV, p. 337.

[2] As far as the practice of intercommunion is concerned it seems clear that foreign Protestants were welcomed at Anglican altars, while Anglicans abroad were left to their own discretion in the matter. The evidence for the admission of non-episcopally ordained foreigners to English cures is less clear. Such as it is, it is summarised in the *Apostolic Ministry* (op. cit., pp. 407 ff). The *locus classicus* is the admission of de Laune, a presbyter ordained in Leyden, to a parish in the diocese of Norwich, without re-ordination. Professor Sykes tells me that this was in 1629, and that though his antecedents were well-known he survived the visitations of Bishops White, Corbet, Wren and Montague, the last two being vigorous high churchmen.

[3] Sykes, op. cit., pp. 14–15. Montague, successively Bishop of Chichester and Norwich, shared with Laud the doubtful honour of being the stormiest ecclesiastical figure of the reign of Charles I.

and Laud's chief ecclesiastical rival, who maintained that bishops were not *de jure divino*,[1] and Field, the great apologist, who held the Hieronymian theory of episcopacy and identified the orders of priest and bishop.[2] But between these two extremes there is a recognizable group of Anglicans who are traditionally called the Caroline divines, though for the present purposes they will be seen to include some who were writing before the end of the reign of Elizabeth. Over a period of sixty years they returned over and again to such themes as the origin of the episcopate, its purpose and function as the focus of unity, its universal acceptance for fifteen hundred years in the Catholic Church, and the attitude of Anglicans to those who lacked it. The content of their thought is so homogeneous that the rest of this essay will take the form of a study of these themes, based on the works of successive writers; a glance at the footnotes will reveal how widely held in this period were the views quoted.

Of these divines, while it is possible that some were more learned, it is certain that none was more painful than Thomas Bilson, Bishop of Winchester. It fell to him in his *Perpetual Government of Christ's Church* (1593) to undertake the first close study of the origins of the episcopate. He found, as did Andrewes and Overall after him, that the principles of hierarchical government were laid down in the Old Testament. From the New he deduces, like Hooker, that, while a part of the 'prerogative and pre-eminence' of the Apostles was limited to their persons and to the duration of their lives, and could not continue, yet 'the moderation of keys and the imposition of hands' were powers which could pass from them to their successors. So he believes 'if the succession of episcopal power came from the apostles to (the first bishops), and so to their successors, we shall conclude that bishops came from the apostles'.[3] Similarly in 1654 Bramhall wrote 'we believe episcopacy to be at least an Apostolical

[1] cf. A. J. Mason, *The Church of England and Episcopacy* (Cambridge, 1914), p. 147. This book is an extended examination of the views on episcopacy of Anglican divines from the sixteenth until the end of the nineteenth century.

[2] Field, *Of the Church*, (ed. 1847), pp. 318–23.

[3] Bilson, *Perpetual Government*, (ed. 1842), pp. 156–7 and 302. cf. Andrewes, *A Summary View of the Government of the Old and New Testament* (L.A.C.T. Minor Works), pp. 339 ff. Overall, *Convocation Book* (L.A.C.T.), p. 125.

institution, approved by Christ himself in the Revelation, ordained in the infancy of Christianity as a remedy against schism; and we bless God that we have a clear succession of it.'[1]

It seems to have been Bilson who first coined the phrase 'apostolic succession': 'they can have no part of the apostolic commission, that have no show of apostolic succession'. Here he was speaking of succession of function; elsewhere he means by the phrase an orderly succession in place: 'This singularity of one pastor in each place descended from the apostles . . . in all the famous churches of the world by a perpetual chair of succession doth to this day continue.'[2] The idea of succession in fact appears surprisingly little in the thought of the sixteenth and seventeenth divines. Where it does appear it would seem to be always in reference to succession in function, place or doctrine, as when Overall says 'of which succession of bishops, whilst the succession of truth continued with it, the ancient Fathers made great account.'[3] Succession of ordination is either ignored or treated as an explicitly Roman doctrine.[4]

The origin of episcopacy, and its continuance through the centuries, having been established, it was necessary now to prove, against the exclusive claims of Rome, that the Church of England followed in the matter, and had always followed, the customs established by tradition in the Church. This task was first undertaken by Francis Mason in his *Consecration of the Bishops in the Church of England*. Mason is usually considered a representative of the more Protestant wing of the Church, and his thought about such things as the nature of the Church and of its sacraments certainly confirms this estimate, but the way in which he undertook the specific task he set himself places him in the succession of the

---

[1] Bramhall, *Works* (L.A.C.T.), vol. I, p. 271. *A Just Vindication of the Church of England*.
[2] Bilson, op. cit., pp. 162 and 319–20.
[3] Overall, op. cit., p. 148.
[4] cf. Thorndike, *Works* (L.A.C.T.), vol. I, pt. II, p. 591: 'The distinction which the Church of Rome is usually answered with is to be admitted, between succession of persons and succession of doctrine.' The question 'What is meant by succession?' is treated by H. F. Woodhouse in *Theology* for October 1952.

'Caroline' divines and affords additional proof that that party was representative of a large section of the seventeenth century church. His book is cast in the form of an imaginary dialogue between a Romanist and an Anglican; more than once his method is first to deny the principles underlying the Roman attack on Anglican validity, and then to prove that the Church of England can stand even if these principles are allowed. On these lines he examines the succession to their sees and the consecration of every living Anglican bishop, providing therewith exhaustive pedigrees. To the consecration of Archbishop Parker he pays particular attention, examining in turn 'the place, the persons, the matter, the form of his consecration'.[1] For the first time the record of that consecration, so carefully preserved in Parker's Register at Lambeth, was published and so brought to the forefront of the controversy about Anglican orders. When the question of succession is being debated he turns on his Roman opponent: 'It is one thing to make a catalogue of bishops succeeding one to another; and another to plot out the chain of their successive ordination. This is the thing you require at our hands, can you perform it? If not by your own sentence you must be put from your priesthood. . . . Seeing that you accuse us of breaking the golden chain, behold it is in your hand, examine it from end to end, look upon every link.'[2] Thus by implication he too rejects the tactile theory of apostolic succession, and in words which have a strangely modern ring. This interesting writer also has the perspicacity to foresee that, other Roman objections having failed, they will fall back on that of defective intention.[3] The Nags Head fable and similar papal arguments, however, were not so easily laid, and other Anglicans had to repeat Mason's painstaking work, notably Cosin and Bramhall during their exile under the Commonwealth.

Another writer who does not neatly fit into the Caroline matrix is the moderate Joseph Hall, Bishop of Exeter, whom W. K. Jordan calls 'perhaps the ablest Anglican thinker in

[1] Francis Mason, *Of the Consecration of Bishops in the Church of England* (ed. 1613), p. 132.
[2] ibid., p. 43.   [3] ibid., p. 41.

the first half of the century'.[1] Encouraged by Laud, he had
in 1637 produced his *Episcopacy by Divine Right Asserted*, a
livre de circonstance occasioned by the renunciation by Bishop
Graham, of Orkney, of his episcopal functions in favour of
the Presbyterian system. Mention of the Northern Kingdom
at this date serves to remind us of the storm cloud gathering
there and ready to burst with such dire effect over the Church
in England. Graham's defection elicited from Hall, moderate
though he was, words for the Genevan system and those who
'hatched' it *[sic]* as harsh as any yet written.[2] Not content
with apostolic origins for the episcopate, Hall traces it back
to the *fiat* of Christ: 'if the foundation were laid by Christ,
and the walls built up by his Apostles, the fabric can be no
less than divine. . . . When Christ and his Apostles give us the
text, well may the Apostolical and Universal Church yield
us the commentary.'[3] But, despite his anger over the particular case in question, he is also concerned to frame the excuses
possible for those reformed churches which have not incorporated the divinely instituted episcopate into their systems.
Unlike Hooker, he felt that Christ and the Apostles having
instituted the three-fold ministry, the Church was in no
position to change it: 'So then the change being made by the
Apostles themselves . . . they being infallibly guided by the
spirit of God, though they changed we may not.' But on the
other hand he takes his cue from Hooker in excusing a
change due to, and springing from, 'inevitable necessity'.
The foreign Protestants (unlike the Scots whom he was
addressing) could not avoid discarding episcopacy at the
Reformation, and only did so unwillingly: 'acts done out of
any extremity can be no precedents for voluntary and deliber-
ate resolutions. . . . They were forced to discard the office, as
well as the men; but yet the office, because of the men; as
Popish, not as bishops: and to put themselves, for the present,
into such a form of government, as under which they might
be sure, without violent interruption, to sow the seeds of the

[1] W. K. Jordan, *The Development of Religious Toleration in England*, vol. II,
p. 147.
[2] Hall, *Works* (ed. 1808), vol. IX, p. 508.
[3] ibid., p. 522 and p. 563.

saving and sincere truth of the Gospel.'[1] This argument from necessity is a recurrent theme in the works of the Caroline divines, Thorndike even elaborating it to demonstrate how the excuse which was valid for foreign Presbyterians was invalid for those at home: the shortcomings of the former are verily due to necessity, but those of the latter only to 'pride and presumption' since in England there existed already at the time of their schism a reformed church.[2]

Hall, not content with apostolic, had insisted on dominical origins for episcopacy. Another writer, who forsook Hooker's cautious principles and insisted on immutable dominical legislation for the office, was Jeremy Taylor. Like Hall he found a distinction in the Gospels between the commission and powers of the seventy and of the twelve.[3] He urges, as again does Hall, that this insistence on the dominical ordering of the Church is the only one likely to impress the Puritans, who give no credence to ecclesiastical tradition.[4] But here the similarity to Hall ends: Taylor had no time for the defensive argument of inevitable and inculpable necessity. 'But then,' he says, 'are all ordinations invalid which are done by mere presbyters without a bishop? What think we of the reformed churches? For my part I know not what to think. . . . We were glad at first of abettors against the errors of the Roman Church; we found these men zealous in it; we thanked God for it, as we had cause: and we were willing to make them recompense by endeavouring to justify their ordinations, not thinking what would follow upon ourselves; but now (1642) it is come to that issue that our own episcopacy is not thought necessary, because we did not condemn the ordinations of their presbytery. Why is not the question rather what we think of the primitive church than what we think of the reformed churches?' Yes, indeed, and the united evidence of the primitive church is against the Presbyterian

---

[1] ibid., p. 601 and p. 517.
[2] Thorndike, *Works* (L.A.C.T.), vol. V, p. 430. He goes on to add that 'many of their own learned and religious men' have declared in favour of episcopacy, an argument repeated by Bramhall, *Works* (L.A.C.T.), vol. II, p. 70.
[3] Jeremy Taylor, *Episcopacy Asserted, Works* (ed. 1853), vol. V, p. 27, cf. Hall op. cit., p. 548.
[4] Taylor, op. cit., p. 33, cf. Hall, op. cit., p. 563.

system. 'In this particular we must have strange thoughts of scripture and antiquity, or not so fair interpretation of the ordinations of reformed presbyteries: but for my part I had rather speak a truth in sincerity, than err with a glorious correspondence.' When considering the argument of necessity, he finds, upon examination of their own writers, that it is not necessity but choice which makes the reformed orders what they are: 'Will not necessity excuse them who could not have orders from orthodox bishops? . . . There were many archbishops that joined in the Reformation, whom they might, but did not, employ in their ordinations; and what necessity then can be pretended in this case I would fain learn, that I might make their defence.' What is worse, he knows that it is their practice to reordain, if the case arise, any episcopally ordained priest who seeks entry to their own presbyteries. The conclusion seems clear, though he cannot bring himself to underline it: 'Shall we then condemn those few of the reformed churches whose ordinations always have been without bishops? No indeed, that must not be; they stand or fall to their own master. And though I cannot justify their ordinations, yet what degree their necessity is of, what they desire of episcopal ordinations may do for their personal excuse, and how far a good life and a catholic belief may lead a man in the way to heaven, although the forms of external communion be not observed, I cannot determine.'[1] To such an impasse was Jeremy Taylor led by his desire, falling for the temptation which Hooker had resisted, to answer the Presbyterians on their own ground. The theory of inculpable necessity had always been a bruised reed, in his hands it broke.[2]

But there was in the seventeenth century, another Anglican approach to the problem of schism, where it focussed on the question of non-episcopal orders. It was most clearly stated by Lancelot Andrewes. As an official anti-Roman apologist it

---

[1] ibid, pp. 118–21.
[2] It should however be noted that elsewhere Taylor seems to modify these opinions in a more liberal direction, saying 'to deny to communicate with those with whom God will vouchsafe to be united . . . because they have not all our opinions and believe not every thing necessary which we overvalue, is impious and schismatical.' ('Liberty of Prophesying', *Works*, vol. V, p. 601.)

was he who expressly formulated the classical Anglican appeal to the two testaments, the three creeds, the first four general councils and the first five centuries of the undivided Church. On this basis he was quite clear that, on the subject of the episcopate, 'our Church doth hold, there is a distinction between bishop and priest, and that *de jure divino*'.[1] This statement he was ready to support by a mass of learned exegesis to prove that the apostles appointed the first bishops in their own life-time. When considering the question of non-episcopal orders, in replying to his French interrogator Du Moulin, he first of all advances the argument of necessity: 'You ask if your churches do not err in the divine law. No, I say. I say that some part of the divine law is missing from your churches: but the blame is not yours, but the hardness of the times. Because you did not have in France kings as favourable to the cause of reformation, as we had in England.'[2] But, while evidently allowing this argument, he has another up his sleeve. 'Nevertheless if our form (i.e. episcopacy) be of Divine right, it doth not follow from thence that there is no salvation without it, or that a Church cannot consist without it. He is blind who does not see Churches consisting without it; he is hard-hearted who denieth them salvation. We are none of those hard-hearted persons; we put a great difference between these things. There may be something absent in the exterior regiment, which is of Divine right, and yet salvation be to be had.'[3] The distinction, here implied by Andrewes, between the being and the divine fullness of a Church, would seem to spring from his earlier insistence that, despite all he has said about the divine right of episcopacy, it is after all not a matter of faith but of order.[4] The distinction had already been noted in the thought of Whitgift,[5] and it appears in that of Mason,[6] but it is the great exiles Bramhall and Cosin

---

[1] Andrewes, *Answer to Cardinal Perron* (L.A.C.T. Minor Works), p. 29.
[2] Andrewes, *Letter to Du Moulin* (L.A.C.T. Opuscula), p. 211 (My translation).
[3] ibid, p. 191. (Bramhall's translation.)
[4] ibid, p. 187. 'Nec tamen, quia divini juris sunt, ideo fidei capita dicenda sunt. Ad agenda Ecclesiae, spectant haec; ad credenda autem aut capita fidei, non nisi improprie, revocantur.'
[5] See above, p. 4.
[6] Francis Mason, op. cit., p. 21.

who develop it to the full. Bramhall, for instance, quotes the above passage from Andrewes with approval and adds a gloss about 'distinguishing between the true nature and essence of a Church, which we do readily grant (the foreign reformed churches), and the integrity or perfection of a Church, which we cannot grant them without swerving from the judgement of the Catholic Church.'[1] Elsewhere this convinced Catholic says, 'I like (the distinction) well . . . the essence of things are unalterable, and therefore the lowest degree of saving faith, of ecclesiastical discipline, of sacramental communion, is sufficient to preserve the true being of a Church.'[2] Cosin makes the same distinction when justifying his communicating with the French Protestants at Charenton, claiming that 'the act (of eucharistic consecration) which they do, though it be disorderly done, and the ordinations which they make, though they make them unlawfully, shall not be altogether null and invalid.'[3]

It may be said of these Anglican exiles, Cosin and Bramhall, and of Herbert Thorndike, who remained in England, that their 'singular praise is to have done the best things in the worst times, and hoped them in the most calamitous.'[4] The plight in which they found themselves adds poignancy and interest to their writings. At home the Church of England was dispossessed; abroad it was surrounded by the threatening machinations of the Roman Catholics at the pathetic court of Charles II. It must indeed have seemed on the point of being crushed between the upper and nether millstones. Yet, defending themselves on two fronts, these writers produced undaunted a stream of works of learning, vision and authority.[5]

There can be no doubt that it was the fact of schism which most concerned them, and the knowledge that the Church of England was blamed for it by both Protestant and Roman Catholic, which most troubled them. The scandal of dis-

<hr />

[1] Bramhall, *Works* (L.A.C.T.), vol. III, p. 518.
[2] Bramhall, *Works* (L.A.C.T.), vol. II, p. 25.
[3] Cosin, *Letter to Mr. Cordel*, op. cit., p. 403.
[4] Epitaph to Sir Robert Shirley who, during the Commonwealth, built a church at his home, Staunton Harold.
[5] See Robert S. Bosher, *The Making of the Restoration Settlement*, pp. 62–7.

unity was never far below the surface for any thinker in the first century after the Reformation, but the handful of loyal and catholic-minded Anglicans who, during the Commonwealth, fought what looked like a rearguard action for their principles, were particularly vulnerable in the matter. For that reason, perhaps, they reply to their accusers with all the more vigour. Bramhall, for instance, countered attacks from Rome by insisting that it was the Romans themselves who were to blame for the fragmentation of Christendom: 'It is not the separation, but the cause, that makes a schismatic. . . . It was not the Protestants that left the communion of the Church of Rome, but the Court of Rome that thrust all the English nation . . . out of their doors, and chased them away from them.'[1] In this and in similar passages the voice, and the influence, of Jewel can be heard echoing across the century.

If Jewel finds a disciple in Bramhall, it was upon Thorndike, of all the seventeenth-century writers, that Hooker's mantle fell. All the themes so far enumerated are summed up and restated with masterly insight in his works. The strength and the weakness of the claims not only of the Romans and the Presbyterians, but also of the Independents, who by now in England held the field, are examined, and the Church of England shown to be unique in taking its stand on Scripture, reason and tradition. Reason it is which counters both the absolute reliance of Rome on the Church, and that of the Independents on Scripture: 'The pretence of infallibility in the Church on the one side, the pretence of the Word and the Sacraments for marks of the Church on the other side, I hold equally frivolous; as equally declaring a resolution never to be tried by reason.'[2] Tradition gave the lie to those Presbyterians who advanced the specious view that 'the unity of the Reformation cannot be preserved but by dissolving the order of bishops among us.'[3] For how could the Church of England so lightly discount the unanimous witness of centuries of Catholic practice: 'if the rank of bishops over their

[1] Bramhall, *Works*, vol. I, p. 128.
[2] Herbert Thorndike, *Works* (L.A.C.T.), vol. II, pt. I, p. 5.
[3] ibid., vol. I, pt. 2, p. 575.

presbyters be . . . estated in possession of sixteen hundred years . . . let me have leave to think it will be hard to show a better title of human right for any estate upon the earth.'[1]

Thorndike was always harking back to the problem of the reunion of Christendom, and to the fundamental issues of that problem: 'The meaning of that article of our creed which professeth one Catholic Church . . . either signifies nothing, or it signifies that God hath founded one visible church; that is, that He hath obliged all Churches (and all Christians . . .) to hold visible communion with the whole Church.'[2] He recognized that all are involved in the sin of schism, and bitterly castigated the Romans for their practice of re-baptism. He recognized too that if unity was to be regained it could only be on the basis of episcopacy. He continually stressed the prime importance of the episcopate, partly for the empirical reason that without its retention there could never be any hope of ultimate reunion with Rome: 'I am satisfied that the differences upon which we are divided cannot be justly settled upon any terms, which any part of the whole Church shall have any just cause to refuse, as inconsistent with the unity of the whole Church';[3] but more than that, as a theologian he saw in the episcopate the God-given focus of unity and seat of authority in the Church. This thought occurs over and over again in his writings. 'I have showed and shall show (episcopacy) to have been in force from the time of the apostles; having first showed that the visible unity of the Church is a thing commanded by God', and based on the communion of dioceses governed by bishops. 'From the beginning the unity of the Church hath been maintained by the mutual intelligence and correspondence of the chief churches . . . always addressed and managed by the heads of the said Churches.'[4] Such was the Anglican vision of, and prayer for, Christendom in the seventeenth century; it has not changed in the twentieth.

[1] ibid., vol. I, p. 92. This argument, of the unchallenged witness of fifteen hundred years to episcopal government, is a favourite of the Caroline divines, appearing in the works of Hooker, Bilson, Overall, Hall, Taylor and Bramhall.
[2] ibid., vol. V, p. 27.   [3] ibid., vol. V, p. 27.
[4] ibid., vol. IV, pt. I, p. 366. This argument, too, is a *leit motif*, appearing and reappearing in the thought of Bilson, Overall, Hall, Taylor and Bramhall; cf. Jeremy Taylor 'the bishop is the band and ligature of the Church's unity', op. cit., p. 195.

V

CHURCH ORDER AND REUNION
IN THE NINETEENTH CENTURY

A. B. Webster

The Revisers' Communion

'THE beginning of a new period in Church History.'[1] This
was the comment of Dr. Hort, one of the most learned and
judicious of English nineteenth-century theologians, on a
unique service of Holy Communion celebrated in Westminster Abbey in 1870. 'It was' he said, 'one of those few
great services, which seem to mark points in one's life. There
was nothing to disturb its perfect quietness and solemnity.'[2]
Amongst those who knelt together round the tomb of King
Edward VI were scholars of the Church of England, of the
Church of Scotland and of the English Free Churches. Before
starting on their lengthy labours of revising the Authorized
Version of the Bible they had decided to meet at a common
Eucharist. The idea had been Dr. Westcott's and the celebrant
was Dean Stanley. The Archbishop of Canterbury, Dr. A. C.
Tait, fully approved. He said afterwards that he hoped that
this memorable service might be seen to be 'an omen of a
time not far distant when our unhappy divisions may disappear, and, as we serve one Saviour and profess to believe
one Gospel, we may all unite more closely in the discharge
of those great duties which our Lord has laid on us, of pre-
paring the world for His second coming.'[3]

But there was another point of view. For many churchmen
the Revisers' Communion was 'the Westminster Scandal'.

[1] A. F. Hort, *F. J. A. Hort* (1896), vol. II, pp. 135 ff., for Hort's point of
view.
[2] ibid.
[3] R. T. Davidson, *A. C. Tait* (1891), vol. II, p. 72.

Some of Dr. Pusey's friends were so shocked that they believed that it was their duty to secede from the Church rather than 'to be against their Lord'. In the exaggerated language of contemporary religious discussion, they were 'in despondency and terror about the Church of England . . . lest they should be involved in the guilt of this sacrilegious Communion.'[1] The presence of Dr. Vance Smith, a Unitarian scholar, amongst the communicants, was certainly an anomaly. Dr. Smith himself had hesitated, and explained in justification that he came because he was glad to confess himself 'a Christian disciple in communion, at least for that occasion'.[2]

Though the more violent discussions centred on the presence of a Unitarian, the crucial question was the propriety of inviting members of the non-episcopal churches to the Anglican communion service. The defenders of the Revisers' Communion, Archbishop Tait and Doctors Westcott, Lightfoot and Hort felt that on this point the objectors had no case. For so vital a task as the revision of the Bible all Christians must unite. 'It is strange', wrote Hort, 'that they should not ask themselves what other alternatives were preferable, and what is really lost to any great interest by the union for once of all English Christians round the altar of the Church.'[3] When the Bible itself was being retranslated in the light of modern knowledge by representative Christian scholars it seemed obvious that these defenders of the faith should worship together despite their differences over Church order.

But the hesitations of Dr. Pusey and his friends were as intelligible as the phrasing of some of their protests was absurd. The hesitations were due not only to the traditional tension between the catholic and the protestant elements always present in the post-Reformation English Church, but also to the special circumstances of Anglican history since 1800. If Dr. Hort discerned the beginning of a new period, Dr. Pusey was as anxious that the gains of the immediate

[1] H. P. Liddon, *E. B. Pusey* (1897), vol. IV, p. 231.
[2] R. E. Prothero, *A. P. Stanley* (1893), vol. II, p. 221.
[3] A. F. Hort, *F. J. A. Hort* (1896), vol. II, p. 1.

past should not be lost. High Churchmen suspected that, in spite of all the work of the Oxford Movement, for many English Christians the Church was an optional appendage of the Christian life. Steps towards reunion were suspect if they seemed to compromise the catholicity of the Church of England and the apostolic succession of its ministers. A brief survey of the place of the Church in nineteenth-century Anglican thought will reveal what ground there was for the caution of Dr. Pusey.

Evangelical Indifference

At the beginning of the century the Church of England was isolated from the rest of Christendom. 'We dwelt alone,' wrote Dr. Pusey, 'our island situation a type of our Church, and were content because there seemed no opening for anything beyond. We were scarcely aware that we were rejected by the Western Church, not formally acknowledged by the Eastern, because we were locally separated from both.'[1] One of Dr. Pusey's younger supporters noticed that this isolation led to 'a growing sense of loneliness',[2] but in 1800 the Church was largely indifferent to any concern for reunion. 'It was' as Canon Scott-Holland so well said of later Anglicanism 'snug and smug among the hedgerows, tied up in Elizabethan red tape, smothered under the convention of the establishment, fat with dignities and very scant of breath.' Neither the doctrine of the Church nor the hope of reunion were major concerns for Anglicans.

In 1800 there was one exception to this isolation, but this exception itself underlined the general unconcern about Church order. The Evangelicals, the most energetic group within the Church, were in close touch with the English Free Churches. But this was less a victory for unity than a testimony to the theological outlook shared by Evangelicals and Free Churchmen, that differences in church order were relatively unimportant. The Evangelical scheme of salvation

[1] E. B. Pusey, *A Letter to the Archbishop of Canterbury* (3rd ed., Oxford, p.17), 1842.
[2] J. R. Hope, *The Bishopric of Jerusalem* (1st ed., London, 1841), p. 59.

was well summed up in the characteristic epitaph on John Berridge, Vicar of Everton, which made no reference to the Church amongst all its details about the spiritual life of the departed:

> 'I was born in Sin Feb. 1716,
> Remained ignorant of my fallen State till 1730,
> Lived proudly on Faith and Works for Salvation
>   till 1754
> Admitted to Everton Vicarage 1755.
> Fled to JESUS alone for Refuge 1756.
> Fell asleep in Christ January 22nd 1793.'

Needless to say lack of episcopal government in the Free Churches was no bar to the Vicar of Everton co-operating with them so long as they shared his Evangelical interpretation of Christianity.

Fortunately this negative attitude towards the Church was not universal among Evangelicals. Charles Simeon on the contrary insisted that Church order could not be ignored. His critics described him as more of a Churchman than a Gospelman, and it was very largely through his influence that 'the Evangelical Party established itself within the Church of England and ceased to stray outside it'.[1] But the more typical attitude of Evangelicals was one of indifference about Church order in general and episcopacy in particular. Their great lay-saint William Wilberforce in his *Practical View* urged Christians to cultivate 'a catholic spirit of amicable fellowship' towards all other Christians of whatever sect or denomination 'who differing from them in non-essentials' agree 'in the grand fundamentals of religion'. For Evangelicals the Church was not among the fundamentals.[2]

The Evangelical attitude to Church order weakened their whole position. It was one thing to emphasize the experience of conversion as giving assurance of salvation through faith in the atoning death of Christ; it was fatal to leave a vacuum where the doctrine of the Church should have been. When the Church Missionary Society was founded on 'the Church

---

[1] Charles Smyth, *Simeon and Church Order* (Cambridge, 1940), p. 310.
[2] For a summary of contemporary criticism of this view see A. J. Mason, *The Church of England and Episcopacy* (Cambridge, 1914), p. 419.

principle' but 'not the High Church principle', this convenient formula covered a failure to theologize about the Church which led not a few of the later Evangelicals or their children to abandon the party.

But the Evangelical refusal to treat the Church as a fundamental had one outstanding advantage: it prevented any fictitious personification of the Church at the expense of Him who is the Saviour of the Church as well as of the world. J. B. Sumner, when Bishop of Chester, issued a Charge, which was unjust as a condemnation of the Tractarians, but was valuable as a guide to those who construct doctrines of the Church. 'We may personify a body for the convenience of discourse, and by degrees forget that a community is not a person. And it is worse still if the body which was first personified comes afterwards to be deified. Yet a process of this kind has gone on with regard to the Christian Church. The Church has been first made an abstraction, and then a person and then a Saviour. The Church, thus invested with divinity, has the minister as her visible representative; and he . . . has assumed the place of God.'[1] No doubt the Evangelicals undervalued Church order but their protest against an undue exaltation has a permanent place in Christian thought.

The last comment which Evangelical teaching invites can best be made in some words of Dr. Pusey. While protesting against Bishop Sumner's condemnation of the Tractarians, Pusey recalled another address of the Bishop's the tone of which, he affirmed, was altogether Catholic. This 'furnishes another remarkable instance of what anyone conversant with those of an opposite school continually sees—how much of apparent condemnation of each arises in misapprehension of what is actually held by either'.[2] Despite differences of emphasis which led to frequent and even bitter mutual recrimination, Evangelicals and High Churchmen could continue to serve one Church.

[1] J. B. Sumner, *A Charge* . . . (London, 1842), pp. 32–3.
[2] E. B. Pusey, *A Letter to the Archbishop of Canterbury* (3rd ed., Oxford, 1842), p. 137.

The High Church Approach

The vacuum in the teaching on the Church was filled by
the High Churchmen and the Tractarians, whose works need
to be carefully distinguished. The three most substantial
books on the Church from the High Church party were
Charles Daubeny's *Guide to the Church* (1798), Thomas Sikes'
Discourse on Parochial Communion (1812) and Christopher
Wordsworth's *Theophilus Anglicanus* (1846). All three restated the traditional High Church view that the Church of
England was the reformed Catholic church of the land, all
other Christians being classified either as intruding Romans
or schismatical Free Churchmen. Sikes' work was uninfluen-
tial and Daubeny's, although the most popular, was marred
by theological intransigeance. (Like some other High Churchmen, Daubeny believed that Free Church baptism was invalid and even doubted whether children baptized by Free
Church ministers might be buried in a churchyard.)[1] The
most authoritative of the three works was Christopher
Wordsworth's largely forgotten *Theophilus Anglicanus*, commissioned by the Archbishop of Canterbury and the Bishop
of London to steady the Church after the departure of Newman. Tedious in style and perverse in arrangement, it is still
suggestive when dealing with the problem of reunion with
Free Churchmen. Dr. Wordsworth was a master of the
classical Anglican theological method, appealing to Scripture and tradition, and finding in the Bishops and Pastors—
particularly when convened in Councils or Synods—the
living interpreters and executors of the faith. Though these
guides of the Church were not infallible, that did not mean
that the Church, and particularly the Bishops, was not to be
obeyed. Episcopacy in fact was a necessary form of government, for in Hooker's words 'if *anything* in the Church's
government, surely the first institution of Bishops was from
heaven, even of God; the Holy Ghost was the Author of it.'[2]
Bishops were the divinely instituted successors and representatives of the Apostles. The Church of England was linked

---

[1] For another case of this belief see the case of Escott *v.* Martin and the
Bishop of Exeter's comments thereon in his *Charge* . . . (London, 1842), pp. 47–74.
[2] C. Wordsworth, *Theophilus Anglicanus* (London, 1873 ed.), p. 89.

to the undivided Church and had 'reformed herself in order to become more truly and soundly Catholic both in doctrine and in discipline'.[1] On the retention of episcopal succession, which appeared to ally the Church of England with Rome over against the Protestants, Wordsworth again quoted Hooker. The Church was resolved to 'follow the perfection of them that like her not rather than the defect of them whom she loves'.[2]

Thus far Wordsworth was restating the traditional Anglican account of the Church as the reformed catholic church of the land. He then made a claim that would have seemed irrelevant to the Evangelicals and dangerous to the Tractarians: that it was the duty of kings and states to promote the true faith even if this involved the risk of state interference with the Church. 'It would be unpatriotic, unloyal and unChristian to desire on that account that the State should be without the power of exercising the noblest and best of her functions, that of promoting the glory of God and the welfare of the People by religious acts.'[3] But the state was no longer Anglican. By welcoming state action to promote the glory of God Wordsworth was bound to recognize the millions of Free Churchmen and the smaller number of Roman Catholics as in some sense members of the Church.

Wordsworth met this difficulty by arguing that the Church of England was the spiritual mother of all Christians in the country, that dissenters were children of the Church though not obedient children. He insisted that Free Church baptism was none the less baptism, despite the absence of episcopal orders. He reminded his fellow Anglicans that 'many schismatics are not such either wilfully or willingly, but only by the circumstances of birth or education, or by neglect on the part of Ministers of the Church; and even they, who *are* so, are still men and Christians and as such they profess to obey the voice of Christ. . . . And though *they* are schismatical, yet she is Universal; and she therefore regards them as still hers, though their schism is not hers.'[4] Wordsworth reached

[1] ibid., p. 208.
[2] ibid., p. 193.
[3] ibid., p. 250.
[4] ibid., p. 258.

the remarkable conclusion that in order to have a high doctrine of the Church he must also have a high doctrine of the State and this involved him in claiming that all Christian citizens were in the relationship of children to their mother the Church of England. True they were disobedient children —a term which a Free Churchman would hardly relish— but they were children for whom a truly Catholic Church must find a place. Wordsworth realized that High Church principles involved some recognition of separated Christians who lacked the historic episcopate. They were not wheat, they were tares but tares, as Wordsworth pointed out with pedantic documentation, are really a bad kind of wheat.[1] They grew in the Church's field, and a wise, charitable Catholic Church would take account of them as Christians.

This thesis endeavoured to do justice at once to Anglican tradition and at the same time to be relevant in nineteenth-century England where so many Christians were not Anglicans. It has been far outpassed by the more brilliant style and more uncompromising claims of the Tractarians but after the passing of a century *Theophilus Anglicanus* has merits we do not find in the Tracts. Unlike the Tracts, it was at once patriotic, reformed and empirical.

Protest from Oxford

Wordsworth and other High Churchmen of the old school had done their best, but a more compelling restatement of the doctrine of the Church, in the face of growing Radical hostility, was made by the Oxford Movement. With an almost fanatical insistence the Tractarians seized on the primary need of the Church to base itself on its spiritual claims and on nothing else. They were brilliantly successful. 'Thank God!' wrote one critical bishop before he began 'unravelling the web of sophistry' in Tract 90, 'the Church is no longer the watchword of a party.'[2] Previously, as Tract 4 acidly but accurately observed, 'we have spoken much in the same tone, as we might, had we been mere Laymen, acting for ecclesi-

[1] ibid., p. 259.
[2] The Bishop of Exeter, *A Charge* . . . (London, 1842), p. 1.

91

astical purposes by a commission under the Great Seal.' On the contrary, the Tractarians pointed out, the Anglican ministry had the commission of the Lord Himself and, as a result, the Church of England was 'the only Church in this realm which has the right to be quite sure that she has the Lord's Body to give to His people'. This assurance was based on the Apostolic Succession of which the hands of the ordaining bishops were the connecting links in the holy chain, a chain which, as a matter of plain historical fact, went back to the Apostles, who had been ordained by Christ. None could be treated as really ordained who had not been thus ordained.

Most modern readers of the Tracts will agree that again and again Newman, Pusey, Keble and their friends asserted the primacy of the spiritual with a compelling sincerity. Respectability, culture, present palpable usefulness and political privileges do not give the pastor his claim on society. No doubt it was true, as Baron von Hügel suggests, that Pusey confined himself unduly to directly religious interests. The Tractarians appeared narrowly academic and ecclesiastical, compared with the old High Churchmen. But this narrowing of interest ensured the clear statement of the truth that the pastors' commission must be given by the heavenly Lord if the pastor is to be, in George Herbert's words, 'the deputy of Christ for the reducing of man to the obedience of God'. This persistent recall to the Gospel as the sole sanction of the Church was the Oxford Movement's great gift to the Church of England.

It was, however, a mixed blessing. An exclusive appeal to the Apostolic Succession as the one test of the Church involved the unchurching of all Protestants at home and in Scotland and most Protestants abroad. Episcopacy was the *esse* of the Church. It is true that in Tract No. 4 it is admitted that though we cannot communicate with Presbyterians or Roman Catholics we do not exclude them from salvation: ' "Necessary to Salvation" and "necessary to Church Communion" are not to be used as convertible terms. . . . What shall we say to the remarkable promise addressed to the Twelve at the Pascal Supper "Ye are they which have continued with me in My temptations; and I appoint unto you a kingdom. . . ." This much no one will hesitate to allow concerning the Apostolic Charter; that it bound all Christians to be loyal and obedient to Christ's Apostles as long as they were living. . . . Is not the *spirit* of the enactment such as renders it incumbent on every one to prefer among claimants to Church authority those who can make out the best title to a warrant and commission from the Apostles.'

The Tracts themselves are the most characteristic but not the sole source for the Tractarians' doctrine of the Church. Both William Palmer of Worcester College and W. G. Ward of Balliol wrote separate treatises but the former's lengthy volumes restate in interminable detail the intolerable judgments which the Tractarian theory involved for non-episcopalians, while the latter's *Ideal of a Christian Church* served only to define the boundary between the Church of England and the Church of Rome. Ward was the spiritual ancestor of those Anglicans who denied an Anglican method in theology and saw the Church of Rome as the only reliable upholder of Catholic truth and Christian holiness. We must not quarrel with Ward's criterion of holiness as a test of the true Church but with his colour blindness, which saw Roman holiness and no other. It was not the criterion but his eccentric result which vitiated his theology.

The Jerusalem Bishopric

In 1841 the King of Prussia and the Archbishop of Canterbury sponsored a scheme which might have been expressly designed to act as a piece of theological litmus paper classifying the existing points of view, Evangelical, High Church and Tractarian. It was critical for many Anglicans. It led F. D. Maurice to produce his most penetrating discussion of the doctrine of the Church and reunion. It was one of the blows which convinced Newman that his own idea of catholicity could not be reconciled with the Church of England, for he and his closest friends were already determined that if any reunion was feasible it was 'our duty that this union should be with Rome' and that Lutheranism and Calvinism were 'heresies just in the same sense in which Pelagianism was'.[1] Everyone recognized that the scheme was much more significant than a missionary device to give episcopal super-intendence to Anglican missions in the Mediterranean, though that was certainly needed.[2] Gladstone was probably right when he wrote many years later that the authorities of the Church of England were deliberately presenting to the public the idea of Catholicity under some other form than the Roman. 'I am now construing events, not relating them; but they are events which it will be the prime duty of the future historian to study, for they have, I think, sensibly affected in its religious aspects the history of this country, nay even of Western Christendom.'[3]

The Jerusalem Bishopric was created in the autumn of 1841 as a joint Anglo-Prussian enterprise on the initiative of Frederick William IV. The three bishops who were appointed before the scheme quietly died in 1881 were nominated alternately by the British and Prussian Crowns, though the Archbishop of Canterbury had an absolute veto on the Prussian nominee. The endowment was provided half by the King of Prussia and half by voluntary subscriptions in England, and the Bishop was given jurisdiction 'over such other Protestant congregations as may be desirous of placing themselves under his authority'. The Bishop was also to have the power of ordaining German ministers on their subscribing to the Confession of Augsburg, and Anglicans and Germans were to use their own liturgies. The King of Prussia intended the Bishopric not only to strengthen the position of his own subjects in Turkey but also to bring together all Protestants. For him it was 'a general Protestant question, when viewed in its connection with the entire Protestant Church'.[4] He hoped that a new era would begin in the history of the Protestant church[5] which, as he wrote to his envoy Baron

---

[1] R. Ornsby, *J. R. Hope-Scott* (London, 1884), vol. I, pp. 304—13.
[2] J. Beaver, *On Intercourse between the Church of England and the Churches of the East* (London, 1840).
[3] R. Ornsby, *J. R. Hope-Scott* (London, 1884), vol. II, p. 281.
[4] W. H. Heckler, *The Jerusalem Bishopric* (London, 1883), p. 27.
[5] ibid., p. 27.

Bunsen in his confidential instructions, must show itself to be a united body.[1]

The scheme was doomed from birth. The bishopric was artificial. So few Christians in Jerusalem were willing to recognize the unfortunate Bishop Alexander on his arrival in the Holy City that if a contemporary print can be relied on, his welcome depended upon some Arab loungers and four uncertain-looking cavalrymen![2] Both Alexander and his two successors were personally unsuitable for so delicate and difficult a task. The German Evangelicals ignored the scheme and did not recognize those who had been ordained in Palestine, while the Prussian state documents made the work of English supporters more difficult by supposing that a union already existed between the German Evangelical Church and the Church of England.[3] But the discussion of the theological implications of reunion under one Anglican bishop was of great interest. Newman issued a protest and Dr. Pusey,[4] William Palmer,[5] Fellow of Magdalen College, and J. R. Hope-Scott,[6] the attractive and very able High Church lawyer, marshalled the arguments against reunion: that the Germans were Protestant and therefore heretical and schismatic, and that the scheme involved a breach of canon law by relaxing confirmation regulations, a canon law which Bishop Alexander himself had sworn to obey. Hope-Scott wrote, 'I had rather that our Church should wait the good providence of God within her present narrow limits, for centuries to come, than that she should gather in whole nations at the expense of even a single Catholic principle.'[7] The scheme was also attacked from the German side as being too friendly to Episcopacy.[8]

The King of Prussia and the Archbishop of Canterbury

[1] ibid., p. 4.
[2] ibid., p. 53.
[3] This is one of the main points in the long anonymous criticism of the scheme, *Examination of an Announcement made in the Prussian State Gazette* (Oxford, 1842).
[4] E. B. Pusey, *A Letter to His Grace the Archbishop of Canterbury* (3rd. ed., Oxford, 1842).
[5] William Palmer, *A Letter to a Protestant Catholic* (Oxford, 1842).
[6] J. R. Hope-Scott, *The Bishopric . . . at Jerusalem* (London, 1841).
[7] ibid., p. 58–9.
[8] W. Hoffmann, *The Anglo-Prussian Bishopric* (London, 1842).

G

did not lack defenders,[1] but by far the most significant discussion was F. D. Maurice's thorough, though characteristically unsystematic, consideration of the Church's attitude towards reunion. Maurice's *Three Letters to the Reverend W. Palmer*[2] begin with a discussion of Catholicism and Protestantism, insisting that an Anglican must be both a Protestant and a Catholic. He must assert that the living Centre of the Church is nothing but Christ Himself. 'I am a Protestant just because I do acknowledge this Catholic centre, and that moment I relinquish my Protestantism, that moment I abandon the best hope for the unity of the Church.'[3] The Papacy had committed a 'mighty practical heresy' by invading the true constitution of the Church and above all by subordinating sacraments, Bible and bishops to its own authority. The Reformation had rightly protested against this 'but now by the awful demonstrations of the French Revolution and by the parody of Christian fraternization which the actors in it were allowed to present, God has been showing us . . . that our business is . . . chiefly to enquire . . . upon what terms and conditions He has constituted society'.[4] As Maurice was never tired of insisting, the Church was human society in its normal state and in this new era it must present itself not as a 'mere utterer of dogmas' but 'as the witness and embodier of those permanent realities which earnest hearts feel that they need and which, when set forth, will be denied at last only by those who deny their own moral being and responsibility. . . . I believe that when any part of the Church is able to assert this position, grounding its own existence simply on the Incarnation of Christ and putting forth all those institutions and ordinances which it has in common with Christendom as the declaration of this Incarnation and of Christ's Headship over the Church, that part of it may be blessed by God to be the restorer of unity to the East and to the West . . .'[5]

In his second letter on *The English Church* Maurice restated his conviction that it was possible for the Church of England

---

[1] e.g., Especially: W. F. Hook, *Reasons for Contributing Towards the support of an English Bishop at Jerusalem* (London, 1842), and A. P. Percival, *A Vindication. . .*, (London, 1843).

[2] London, 1842.   [3] ibid., p. 7.   [4] ibid., p. 13.   [5] ibid., p. 15.

and for any other portion of the Church to be most Catholic when it is most Protestant. He set out at some length the terms of union which might be proposed for the various Churches—Roman, Orthodox and Continental Protestant. In the case of the continental Protestants Maurice insisted that we cannot reunite simply because we both protest against Rome and because we hold the same doctrines about personal justification. 'That which is the bond of fellowship with the Christians of other nations must be something which is not national, nor individual but universal. . . . Now Bishops being as we believe the witnesses and representatives of Christ's universal kingdom are the very instruments of our communion with other nations. . . . We cannot then recognize a Church without Bishops. We cannot do it for our own sakes, because we believe we have a solemn trust and responsibility to uphold this great universal institution of Episcopacy; because we believe that it has been preserved to us in a wonderful manner for the last three centuries, when there was scarcely anything in our minds to make it intelligible; because we believe that all the circumstances of this age are declaring to us its purpose and its necessity. And we cannot do it for your sakes. We will not use the name of charity, when we have rejected the thing. Now it is not charity to tell you that you have not lost in a great measure the sense of being members of a Catholic body, for your wisest men know you have. It is not charity to tell you that you have any means of resisting the *appearance* of a Catholic Church which there is among the Romanists; for the practical power of Romanism in Germany, and in every country of the Continent, together with the desertion of your own poets and artists to it, prove that you have not. . . . It is therefore not charity to tell you that you can dispense with an institution, which if received livingly and practically, in the way in which we believe that you have been prepared by God's discipline and grace to receive it, as the witness and not the substitute for Christ's presence, might be the remedy for all these evils.'[1] Maurice concluded his second letter by urging that we should rejoice when the continental Protestant

[1] ibid., p. 35–6.

97

gloried in his reformation fathers and his present church. 'Let us rejoice to hear him call what seems to us but the fragment of a Church by that great and glorious name.' Still less should we attack his national feeling: 'It is as much as saying that we want him to be an Anglican, which he cannot be, and not a Catholic, which he can.'[1]

Maurice's Third Letter naturally concluded that the scheme involved no compromise of Catholic principles and that the English bishops could not have rejected the invitation to form the Jerusalem bishopric. The scheme recognized Christ's Headship of the Church and expressed it by the acknowledgement of a bishop. This was the grand fundamental of all Church order in face of which Dr. Pusey's objection that German Protestants prayed sitting down and Hope-Scott's insistence on all canons being always obeyed could be ignored. If episcopacy was actually established, if the creeds and the eucharist were retained, there could be no objection to practices being permitted in the Church in Jerusalem which would be irregular for an Anglican in England.

This thorough discussion had important consequences in clarifying the Anglican attitude to reunion. It was made clear that the days of isolation were over. Lambeth recognized that co-operation with continental Protestants was essential and took up again the work of Cranmer and Wake, who had both negotiated for reunion. It also became clear to Newman, J. R. Hope-Scott and W. Palmer of Magdalen that for those who believed that reunion with Rome was the way ahead and that all Protestants were heretics, there was no place in the Church of England. Other Anglicans looked forward to reunion with a new enthusiasm and did not despair of reconciliation with other Christians, so long as episcopacy, as understood in the Preface to the Ordinal, was maintained. But Dr. Pusey and his many supporters, who had done most to recover the sense of the Church, were in a difficult position. They had rejected the scheme and continued to protest against any actions which implied that the Protestants had a Church. Episcopacy was so essential to the

[1] ibid., p. 38–9.

being of a Church that no negotiations ought to take place with those who lacked it. This Tractarian view effectively closed the door against any advance towards reunion with Protestants at home or abroad and began to threaten the Church of England with a new form of isolation based not on complacent indifference but on theological principle. It was this attitude which led to the widespread condemnation of the Revisers' Communion and to a hesitant approach towards the Ecumenical Movement. But fortunately for the Church of England many of those who most valued the work of Dr. Pusey and the Tractarians began a gradual modification of their attitude to episcopacy and reunion.

The Modification of the Tractarian View

English theological discussions before 1850 have an attractive simplicity. The critical study of the Bible, of the age of the Fathers and of the period of the Reformation had scarcely begun in this country. It was possible to state without any second thoughts that Christ appointed the apostles, the apostles appointed the bishops and the bishops consecrated other bishops down to the present day. But once the new approach was fully used every Christian doctrine was bound to be affected. This was far from obvious at first. Charles Gore, the first Principal of Pusey House, Oxford, accepted the critical approach to the Old Testament but stopped short of applying it to the New, still less to the doctrine of the Church. He wrote in 1888 with all the assurance of the Tractarian theory: 'It is absolutely certain that for a large number of centuries it had been understood beyond all question that only Bishops could ordain . . . it follows then—not that God's grace has not worked and worked largely through many an irregular ministry where it was exercised in good faith, but—that a ministry not episcopally received is invalid, that is to say that it falls outside the conditions of covenanted security and cannot justify itself in terms of the covenant.'[1]

This unchurching of all who lack the Apostolic Succession has become more and more unsatisfactory. Not only has

[1] Quoted with significant comments by J. K. Mozley, *Some Tendencies in British Theology* (London, 1951), p. 66.

there been a gradual recognition of the place of the Church amongst Protestants, which makes it absurd to assert that they undervalue what they so eagerly claim, but critical studies have tended to weaken the theory of a simple chain of hands. Sir Edwyn Hoskyns, writing in *Essays Catholic and Critical*—the avowed successor of Gore's own *Lux Mundi*—insisted that the 'unity between Christ and the Church, vital though it is for the Catholic religion, raises a historical problem as delicate as it is important; delicate because of its extreme complexity.'[1] Dr. Darwell Stone, a successor of Dr. Gore at Pusey House, recognized that Anglican formularies do not assert that outside the Apostolic Succession there is no valid ministry. At the Reformation 'the Church of England carefully required that only the episcopally ordained should minister, while in Article XXIII a phrase was chosen which did not explicitly commit those who subscribed to it to assert the necessity of episcopal ordination. . . . Those who held a theoretical opinion that episcopacy is not necessary were within their rights in availing themselves of the loophole in Article XXIII, provided they recognized what was required in practice.'[2] For an exclusive doctrine of Apostolic Succession as of the *esse* of the Church 'any reference to the 16th and 17th century English formularies and divines is a broken reed for anything except the practical requirements.'[2]

The implications of these critical and historical studies, unknown to the seventeenth-century Carolines or to the nineteenth-century Tractarians, have led to gradual modifications of the Tractarian scheme among 'Catholic' Anglicans such as T. A. Lacey, E. J. Bicknell and Frank Weston. (The views of theologians of greater calibre such as O. C. Quick and William Temple, who reached the same conclusions, are of less significance here since they owed more to F. D. Maurice than to Pusey.) In 1917 Canon T. A. Lacey argued that 'schismatics who confess Christ must be included within the Church. . . . And this may lead us to the humbling thought

---

[1] *Essays Catholic and Critical* (London, 1926), p. 153.
[2] F. L. Cross, *Darwell Stone* (London, 1943), p. 235–6.
[3] ibid., p. 244.

that we are all more or less schismatic. If not wilfully then by misfortune or by the fault of others we are divided from one another. Yea, Christ is divided.'[1] Two years later Dr. Bicknell, also writing from the Catholic point of view, asked 'How then does the Church of England regard Non-Conformist ministrations? Stress should be laid on the positive rather than on the negative side. We are bound to hold fast to our ministry to secure the validity of our own ministrations. But the true antithesis to "Valid" in such cases is not "invalid" but rather "precarious". We are convinced that Non-Conformist rites are irregular: they have not on them the stamp of approval of the whole Church. But we have no wish to dogmatize on their position in the sight of God or to deny that He employs them as means of grace. God is not limited to His ordinances but we are. We believe that the maintenance of the succession is God's will for us and a real means towards the reunion of Christendom.'[2] In the following year, at the time of the Lambeth Conference of 1920. Bishop Weston, the outstanding 'Catholic' present, was even prepared to receive whatever any community thought was lacking to his orders.[3]

These have not been merely theoretical discussions. More and more Catholic theologians of the Church have been willing to join in reunion discussions with non-episcopalians with a tolerance which would have surprised the Tractarians. Bishop Talbot of Winchester and Dr. Frere, Superior of Mirfield, attended the Edinburgh Conference of 1910. Bishop Weston, despite all his protests over the Kikuyu controversy, was one of those who inspired the 1920 Lambeth Appeal for Unity. At that conference he was so impressed by the great Indian bishop, Azariah of Dornakal, that he confessed to him, 'If *you* are one of the bishops of the South India United Church I shall be entirely satisfied.'[4] Still more remarkable was the declaration issued from Lambeth in 1923, signed by a number of leading churchmen,

---

[1] T. A. Lacey, *Unity and Schism* (1917), p. 150.
[2] E. J. Bicknell, *Theological Introduction* (1939 ed.), p. 423.
[3] H. M. Smith, *Frank, Bishop of Zanzibar* (1926), p. 234. Weston, however, was an erratic thinker not without his temporary enthusiasm.
[4] ibid., p. 230.

including Talbot and Frere, which stated that Free Church 'ministries which imply a sincere intention to preach Christ's Word and administer the Sacraments as Christ has ordained, are real ministries of Christ's Word and Sacrament in the Universal Church.'[1] In 1933 both Houses of Convocation of Canterbury and York passed acts which permitted the admission of non-Anglicans to Holy Communion on certain specified occasions.[2] Perhaps the climax of this movement was the great Oxford Conference of 1937 when the Archbishop of Canterbury himself celebrated Communion for all the delegates from the many divided Churches.

Dr. E. G. Selwyn, Dean of Winchester, summarized the Tractarian theory and decisively rejected it in a memorable speech in the Lower House of the Canterbury Convocation on 21 January, 1932. 'It had sometimes been said that at the Reformation the plate of the Christian Church was broken to pieces but that the part which had the letter "P" on it for "Pope" must now be regarded as the whole plate. That was really the Roman idea. There was at the beginning of the Oxford Movement a similar Tractarian idea put forward, only it was said that the part with the letter "E" for "Episcopacy" must be regarded as the whole plate and that those who were able to claim episcopacy were the whole Church and the rest were outside. He was quite sure that that attitude was no longer possible.'

Dr. Selwyn was expressing the view of a majority of the spiritual descendants of the Tractarians but not of all. In the present century Bishop Gore, Dr. Darwell Stone and many of the authors of *The Apostolic Ministry* have continued to oppose moves towards reunion. The rather hasty rapprochement of the Kikuyu Conference perhaps deserved the criticism it received but Bishop Gore also distrusted the 1920 Lambeth Appeal. He believed that 'For the most part Non-Conformists have not the fundamental Catholic idea of Church and creed and sacraments and ministry, without which all reunion will be fallacious and impermanent.'[3]

[1] Quoted in Mozley's, *Some Tendencies in British Theology* (London, 1931) p. 66.

[2] *Acts of Convocation* (1948), pp. 117–18.

[3] G. L. Prestige, *Charles Gore* (London, 1935), p. 453.

But perhaps the Nonconformists had moved faster than Gore would allow, perhaps an irenic theology of the Church was more common than he had noticed, perhaps Christians were approaching agreement on the doctrine of the Church— that those essential marks of catholicity and apostolicity do not depend simply on the possession of the Apostolic Succession and yet that the coming great Church will have one episcopate, which has grown out of the historic episcopate of the past.

The process whereby Biblical criticism was accepted by the descendants of the Tractarians provides an analogy which suggests that their doctrine of the Church will be sufficiently modified to allow reunion to go forward. Dr. Darwell Stone was once asked by a correspondent whether Catholics might accept the late date for the Book of Daniel, which was given in the *New Commentary* edited by Dr. Gore, despite Dr. Pusey's preference for the traditional early date. Darwell Stone replied that the later date might be accepted and he continued, 'It is important to remember that when Dr. Pusey wrote the late date was being urged in the interests of unbelief, whereas now believing critics are accepting it. In this way the whole context of the question has been changed.'[1] To-day the whole question of the Church has been changed. No Anglican and not many non-Anglican theologians would regard the Church as an optional appendage or advocate reunion without insisting on episcopacy in the Church of the future. Dr. Pusey could not believe that the Bible could be authoritative if verbal inspiration were abandoned. The Church has rejected verbal inspiration but retained an authoritative Bible. Cannot it now safely reject the Tractarian theory of apostolic succession but retain the belief which that theory was intended to safeguard—that an episcopal church order will alone express the mind of Christ in the Church which is to be?

Conclusion

A brief review of Anglican thought on reunion suggests that Dr. Hort was right when he saw the Revisers' Com-

[1] F. L. Cross, *Darwell Stone* (London, 1943), p. 323.

munion as the symbol of 'a new period in church history'—
a period in which the great Church of the future will be born.
The two views that episcopacy is solely a matter of expediency in the secondary question of church order, and that
episcopacy is essential to the Church since it alone guarantees
the presence of sacramental grace, have both been thoroughly
discussed since 1800. The historic parties within the Church
of England, which have previously been unable to agree
even to differ, seem to be reaching a common mind able to
meet the imperious demands for a united Church at home
and abroad. The crises of the past, the Radical attack on the
Church, the Jerusalem Bishopric, the rise of biblical criticism, the growth of the ecumenical movement, have prepared the Church for the decisions which must soon be taken.

As so often F. D. Maurice can speak for the whole Church
of England. 'If we labour that our Protestant brethren may
unite with us on Catholic principles and for Catholic objects,
we shall find out better than all the doctors can teach us
what Catholicity is, how impossible it is that it can thrive
without Protestantism. We shall not be put to the strange
alternative of forsaking the steps of our fathers, in order that
we may become more humble and reverent; we shall be
able to abide in the Church of our own land, and yet to
believe that THE Church belongs to no land, that our
citizenship is in the Heavens.'[1]

[1] F. D. Maurice, *Three Letters* . . . (2nd ed., London, 1842), p. 75.

VI

THE HISTORIC EPISCOPATE

H. W. Montefiore

By keeping the historic episcopate, the Church of England has preserved a visible sign of continuity that reaches back to the primitive church. Bishops are consecrated into the historic episcopate; priests are ordained into the apostolic succession through the laying on of hands by the bishop; by the bishop the laity are received at confirmation into full membership of the Church of England. Such are the facts. But within the Church of England itself there are differences of interpretation. Controversy within Anglican circles has in the past circled round two main views.

1. The historic episcopate guarantees the church. Without it, *non est ecclesia*. The church derives all its authority from Christ through the historic episcopate, which is the divinely ordained channel of grace. The episcopate has delegated some of its functions to the priesthood, and some to the church as a whole. But only priests who have been ordained into the apostolic succession have authority and grace to celebrate the Eucharist. Non-episcopal bodies are like the proselytes at the gate. Thus Anglicans and Orthodox are within the Covenant, but Methodists and Presbyterians are outside it. Because they lack the historic episcopate, they do not form part of the visible church. They may perhaps belong to the 'soul of the church' but not to the body. Such grace as they receive through their non-episcopal ministries is uncovenanted, although it is none the less real for that.

   'If then we follow the teaching of Scripture and the tradition of the Church we are bound to say that a valid ministry is one which, in accordance with primitive ordering, proceeds in due succession from the apostles by the laying on of hands of the Essential Ministry; and that should such a ministry fail, the apostolic Church, which is the Body of Christ in space and time, would disappear with it . . .'[1]

2. The church is the body of Christ, and all who are baptized into Christ belong to the church, which is the spiritual society of the people of God. Within Christendom the church militant has different branches, some of which have different methods of ordering the church. The historic episcopate has certain obvious advantages. It provides a link of continuity with the past. The bishop is the representative of the church, and his office is strategically important for the strengthening of the faithful and the propagation of the Gospel. Christianity is concerned with personal relationships; and because a man can act in a more personal way than a committee, the bishop is preferable to the presbytery. The bishop can be a father to his clergy and a shepherd to his flock. The diocese which is his special care makes a good unit of ecclesiastical polity. Episcopacy may at times in the past have degenerated into prelacy: nevertheless episcopacy remains the best as well as the most natural method of church government. Some would say that the established Church of England reflects the same genius for representative monarchy as our political constitution. Moreover, tradition has sanctified what common sense has evolved. Those who hold this view naturally tend to equate many of the forms of the church's ministry which are to be found in different branches of the church. Such people may have a very 'high' doctrine of ordination, but decline to see any special religious significance in the ordination of a priest by a bishop into the apostolic succession. For them, this is not a matter of proper *theological* importance.

Apostolicity will be the mark of a church whose testimony to Jesus Christ is the same as that of the Apostles. This and this alone is the element of true continuity in the life of the Church. Changes in organisation, developments in theology and extensions of the range of mission there are bound to

[1] Kirk, *Apostolic Ministry* (Hodder and Stoughton, 1946), p. 40.

be . . . but the Gospel neither grows nor develops. It is the final and sufficient Word of God to men which can be received only on the testimony of the Apostles.[1]

On the former view episcopacy is thought to be of the *esse* of the church, on the latter view it is seen as the *bene esse* of the church. The aim of this essay is to shew that neither of these two views can prevail against the other, for both are wrong. The first is erroneous, the second is inadequate. Previous chapters in this book have reviewed both the teaching of the Bible about the church and ministry, and the views of the early Fathers as well as the attitudes of Anglicans at two important phases of English church history. These demand a third view, that the historic episcopate is of the *plene esse* of the church.

3. All persons baptized into Christ are thereby made members of His church, whether they belong to episcopal or non-episcopal bodies. Lutherans, Presbyterians, Anglicans and Roman Catholics are all members of Christ's church. The full stature of the church is shown by many marks which can in the end be listed under four heads— one, holy, catholic and apostolic. Yet, because all church bodies fail to shew forth in their fullness all four characteristics of the church's nature, all are in some sense deficient. It cannot be denied that some non-episcopal bodies shew forth other marks of the church more fully than the Church of England. It may well be that 'fellowship' is more fully realized within the Methodist rather than the Anglican churches: that the 'priesthood of all believers' has fuller concrete expression in the Presbyterian Church of Scotland than in the Church of England. But the Anglican communion has retained the historic episcopate and with it the priesthood and the diaconate: these belong to the *plene esse* of the church. Whatever, for instance, the Congregational Union has got which the Church of England lacks, it is deficient in this mark of the fullness of the church.

None of the statements of the 'second view' are here

[1] F. J. Taylor, *The Church of God* (London, 1946), p. 136.

denied. But as a basis for episcopacy they are inadequate. The historic episcopate is a matter not only of pastoral but also of direct *theological* importance. It provides the full embodiment of the Gospel in church order. It does this in two respects. Firstly, the historic episcopate provides the effectual sign of unity. It embodies in church order the biblical proclamation that Christ's church is one. Secondly, it embodies in church order the principle of apostolicity. The episcopally ordained ministry is both 'sent' to represent Christ to His church and is representative of the church. It provides the guardianship of the Word and Sacraments, of the faith and the flock of Christ. The historic episcopate is thus an effectual sign of the relation of Christ to His church: for it manifests His authority within His church.

The historic episcopate is therefore the outward means and pledge that Christ's church is one and apostolic. It proclaims that the real nature of the church is given by God, and serves to actualize what it proclaims. It is not, however, a mere matter of the church's outward form. The church is sacramental, and its outward structure embodies grace and spirit. The historic episcopate will be a fully expressive and instrumental sign only in the future re-united church of Christendom. That does not mean that Anglicans can afford to undervalue it in the present, for those who possess the historic episcopate possess something here and now of the fullness[1] of Christ which non-episcopal bodies lack.

In the past much confusion has been caused by failure to distinguish these three different views of the church's ministry. Many Anglicans who have rejected the first view have found themselves arguing for the second in perhaps rather uncongenial company, and vice versa. This essay attempts to shew that the third view is the true one, and that it accords with the main tradition of Anglican authority and belief.

[1] The phrase *fullness of the Church* is used in this essay to express what Bramhall meant by the *perfection of the Church*. The former is preferred because (*a*) *fullness* retains a biblical category and (*b*) *perfection* may imply an ethical flavour which is absent from *fullness*.

The preface to the Ordinal carefully refrains from 'un-churching' non-episcopal bodies, and merely gives historical reasons why episcopal orders are to 'be continued and reverently used in the Church of England'. It is true that the opening rubric of the service for the ordination of priests requires a sermon to declare 'how necessary that Order is in the Church of Christ'. That is as near a definition as the Ordinal comes. It seems to rule out episcopal ministries as a mere method of church government. The Prayer Book, however, is, like the Articles, intentionally vague. It is commonly thought that the word 'necessary' meant in the sixteenth century what it means to-day. The Oxford English Dictionary, however, states that the word had 'in the sixteenth and early seventeenth century use frequently approaching the sense of "useful" without being absolutely indispensable'. Many instances could be quoted of this usage, and it should be remembered that the rubric here under discussion was first composed in the sixteenth century. An interpretation, therefore, of 'necessary' in this rubric which does not equate it with 'indispensable' is philologically sound. When the rubric is read in connection with Articles XIX, XX, XXIII, it surely can only mean that episcopal orders are necessary not for the existence of the church but for its fullness.

The prime fount of Anglican authority, however, is neither liturgy nor formularies, but the Bible.

> Holy Scripture containeth all things necessary to salvation, so that whatsoever is not read therein, or cannot be proved thereby, is not to be required of any man, that it should be believed as an article of the Faith, or be thought necessary or requisite to salvation.[1]

This appeal to the Scriptures is basic to the position of the Church of England, and is not to be gainsaid by any talk of 'general assent' to the XXXIX Articles. The New Testament is the apostolic record of the life of Christ and the apostolic church. The Old Testament is the foreshadowing of the New, and the record of the preparation for the coming

[1] Article VI.

of Christ. The inspiration and the authority of the Bible have been recognized, under the guidance of the Holy Spirit, by the *communis sensus fidelium* within the church. Here is the inspired record of the apostolic church in its wholeness, under the judgment of which stands our present divided church. Just as the life of Christ is the pattern for the individual Christian, so the apostolic record of the church which He founded is normative with regard to essentials, but not with regard to fullness, for the church to-day. The church is not precluded from doing or believing anything which is not found in the New Testament. But nothing *essential* to the life of the church has been omitted from the biblical record. Various attempts have been made to prove from the Bible that episcopacy is essential to the church. They have involved special pleading. They have not won general acceptance. The evidence of the New Testament itself is too scattered, inconclusive and even inconsistent. Our knowledge of the sub-apostolic period is equally fragmentary and uncertain. From the nature of the evidence there can be no clear proof.

What then of probabilities? For the purpose of this essay there is fortunately no need to summarize the conflicting views of the origin of episcopacy that have been advanced in the last fifty or sixty years. They range from the extremes of Döllinger[1] and Schmiedel[2] to the more moderate conclusions of J. B. Lightfoot,[3] Streeter[4] and Harnack.[5] Most of these theories seem to have been forgotten, like regular lines during a summer sale, in the stir caused by the publication of the *Apostolic Ministry*. This is partly due to its massive *façade* of scholarship, partly to the extravagant claims which accompanied it. The authors of this work have reformulated and refurbished a theory of two ministries, an 'essential' and a 'dependent' ministry, which was originally adumbrated

---

[1] *The first age of Christianity and the Church* (London, 1906), p. 292 f.
[2] *Encycl. Biblica.*, Article on Ministry.
[3] Dissertation I, *Commentary on Philippians*, (Macmillan, 1885), p. 227 f. cf. J. A. Robinson in *The Early History of the Church and Ministry* (ed. H. B. Swete, Macmillan, 1918), p. 90 ff.
[4] *The Primitive Church* (Macmillan, 1929), p. 262.
[5] *The Constitution and Law of the Church in the first two centuries* (London, 1910), pp. 32–105.

by Gore.[1] This re-statement is a magnificent *tour de force*, complete with Scriptural arguments (literal and typological), Rabbinic precedents and fresh exegesis of the sub-apostolic age. In fact, it is open to damaging criticism:[2] but, however brilliantly it was propounded, it could never attain to more than probability.

Probability is not enough. Even if the authors of the *Apostolic Ministry* were right about the existence in the primitive church of two kinds of ministry, it would still be impossible to suppose that the so-called 'essential ministry' was really what its name implies. No father would tell his child that it was essential for his safety to take cover in an air-raid shelter without making sure that the child knew both where the shelter was and what it was like. So, if episcopacy were to be essential to the life of the church, God would have made it quite clear to us. He who had condescended to become man for the salvation of the world would not allow the benefits of His passion to be jeopardized by the doubtful hypotheses of biblical scholarship. There can therefore be no support from the Bible that the apostolic succession through the laying on of hands guarantees the church. It may be read into the text, but it cannot be read out of it.

The authority of *tradition* as well as the Bible has been recognized by Anglicans, for while the Bible usually interprets itself, it needs further interpretation by the tradition of the church. The primary meaning of tradition is 'the living stream of the Church's life'.[3] In this sense tradition includes the Bible (and was used by the Fathers as a name for the

---

[1] *The Church and the Ministry* (Longmans, 1919), p. 296. cf. Duchesne, *The Early History of the Christian Church*, vol. I (Murray, 1910), p. 262 ff. and Döllinger, op. cit., p. 262 ff. For a modification of this view, cf. C. H. Turner, *Studies in Early Church History* (Oxford, 1912), p. 24 f.

[2] For criticism by Anglicans, cf. specially *The Ministry of the Church* (Canterbury Press, 1947); *The Apostolic Ministry*, S. L. Greenslade in *Theology*, vol. 50, pp. 82 ff., 134 ff.; *Some Aspects of the New Testament Ministry*, G. W. H. Lampe (S.P.C.K., 1949); *Problems of Reunion*, A. E. J. Rawlinson (Eyre and Spottiswoode, 1950); *The Apostolic Succession in the first two centuries of the Church*, A. Ehrhardt (Lutterworth, 1953), pp. 1–34.

[3] cf. *Fathers and Heretics*, G. L. Prestige, (S.P.C.K., 1940), p. 32.

Bible);[1] for, although the Bible stands in judgment over tradition, it is itself a part of and derived from tradition. There is also a narrower meaning of tradition, which is used here. This denotes all those opinions, beliefs, customs and liturgical practices which may interpret the biblical record but which do not find explicit expression in the Bible. Anglican theologians have given much weight to the writings of the Fathers of the undivided church, and to the findings of the first four ecumenical councils, not because they are interested in antiquity as a zoologist is interested in fossils, but because here can be found the living tradition of the primitive church. Later tradition has not the same value, because the sin of schism saps the authority of the church's witness, and results in mutually inconsistent traditions. (In fact, the value even of primitive tradition is impaired because the church has never been without sin, nor completely undivided: this is one reason why the Church of England claims to give authoritative and reliable guidance but rejects any claim to infallibility.)

If there were evidence to shew that apostolic succession (through the laying on of hands) was regarded in *apostolic* times as essential for the existence of the church, then there would be reason for second thoughts about the interpretation of the scriptural doctrine of the church and ministry. But there is no reliable evidence for such apostolic tradition. A previous essay in this book has shewn how hopeless it is to look for evidence from the tradition of the early Fathers to support the view that episcopacy is of the *esse* of the church. 'When once it is proved,' wrote Salmon,[2] 'that the Church was at any time ignorant of a doctrine, there can be no pretence that the Church, at any subsequent period, derived its knowledge of tradition from Apostolic tradition'. These words were directed against the extreme claims of Roman supremacy, but they are equally applicable to the extreme claims of episcopacy.

Nor can appeal be made on this matter to later tradition

---

[1] For the various senses in which tradition can be used, cf. *Tradition and the Spirit*, D. Jenkins (Faber, 1951), Chapter I; *Spiritual Authority in the Church of England*, E. C. Rich (Longmans, 1953), pp. 131–5.

[2] *The Infallibility of the Church*, G. D. Salmon (Murray, 1899), p. 134.

as 'the developing mind of the church'. Newman saw that episcopacy could be proved neither from Scripture nor from primitive tradition; and he did not attempt to do so. He argued that episcopacy was part of the development which led from the Apostles to Papal Supremacy. 'When the Church was thrown upon her own resources, first local disturbances gave exercise to bishops, and next ecumenical disturbances gave exercise to Popes; and whether communion with the Pope was necessary for Catholicity, would not and could not be debated until a suspension of that communion had actually occurred.'[1] Newman's argument breaks down, because it is impossible to prove, without the additional dogma of papal infallibility, that the development of dogma within the Roman Catholic communion is a right development. Indeed Newman's fellow-travellers, who appeal to the developing mind of the church but who stop short at a belief in the necessity of episcopacy, are left hanging in the air, for they refuse to bolster it with the belief in papal infallibility which Newman was prepared to accept. 'The developing mind of the church' is, however, a fiction. The sin of disunity has effected partial schizophrenia. As Salmon demonstrated,[2] Newman's type of argument could be used to prove the necessity of Protestant instead of Roman Catholic doctrine.

The Bible, tradition—and reason. Dr. Henson defined the principle of the English reformation to be 'a frank acceptance of sound learning as competent to revise current tradition both by interpreting afresh the sacred text, and by certifying through independent research the true verdict of Christian antiquity.'[3] When Richard Hooker fearlessly asserted the reason to be divine, he was making a typically Anglican appeal to the independent use of reason as the third source of authority in religion.

When the claim of episcopacy to be of the *esse* of the church is subjected to the scrutiny of reason it is found wanting.

[1] J. H. Newman, *Essay on Development* (Longmans, 1906), 1878 ed., p. 151.
[2] op. cit., p. 40.
[3] Henson, *The Church of England* (C.U.P., 1939), p. 59, quoted by E. C. Rich, op. cit., p. 40.

Non-episcopal churches hold the apostolic faith as defined in the Creeds with no greater latitude of interpretation than that permissible within the Church of England. Many of England's foremost theologians are biblical scholars belonging to non-episcopal bodies: they are accepted for what they are, Doctors of the church. They are not just 'step-children' of Christ.

> On the doctrines of God the Father, the Person and Work of Christ, the Person and Mission of the Holy Spirit, the Trinity and the Life Everlasting, we have found nothing that separates any of these Communions from another. All acknowledge the apostolic faith as contained in the Scriptures and expressed in the Apostles and Nicene Creed.[1]

Members of the 'Free Churches' are baptized with prayer into the threefold name. By them men and women are brought to acknowledge the rule of God and the Lordship of Christ. They come to a saving knowledge of our redemption in Christ and are taught to lead a christian life in accordance with the teaching of Christ. They enter a tradition of private prayer and corporate worship. Such churches, in England and abroad, have as good a claim to the fruits of the Spirit as the Church of England, some of them with four hundred years of vigorous life behind them. 'These ministries,' declared the Lambeth Conference of 1920,[2] 'have been manifestly blessed and owned by the Holy Spirit as effective means of grace.' In other words, these bodies are part of Christ's church.

To say this is not to minimize the great difference in ways of life and worship between 'protestant' and 'catholic' communions. The frequent partaking of the Holy Communion; the acceptance of the lesser sacraments such as Confirmation and Penance; the practice of mental and affective prayer; a loving awareness of and respect shewn to the Saints and specially to the Mother of Jesus; religious communities; the observance of the church's year and 'joining in the prayer of the church'; the riches of traditional liturgical worship; the traditional methods of self-discipline;

---

[1] *Church Relations in England*, (S.P.C.K., 1950), p. 26.
[2] Appeal to all Christian people (1920), §IX.

retreats: here is a heterogeneous list of some of the distinctive features which comprise the *ethos* of those 'catholic' churches which have retained the historic episcopate. These things do not belong to the essential nature of the church. 'Catholics' believe them to belong to its fullness, just as 'Protestants' believe that they have other elements to contribute to the plenitude of the church.

So far as Holy Communion is concerned, most non-episcopal bodies allow, broadly speaking, the same latitude to differing 'intentions' as is permissible within the Church of England. Some non-episcopal churches have a rite of Holy Communion differing considerably from the Anglican rite. But to call the sacraments of these communions mere 'simulacra'[1] is indeed to wander with Alice through the looking-glass. It implies that, so far as the Eucharist is concerned, ministers who have not been episcopally ordained exercise a ministry which is irregular, invalid and even inefficacious. Such a view not only 'offends against the formed convictions of non-episcopal ministries by seeming to deny them a real ministry and sacramental means of grace'.[2] It also offends against common sense. Reason cannot endorse the claim that non-episcopal bodies do not really partake of Christ through His sacrament because they do not form part of the church.

The view that episcopacy is of the *esse* of the church has been submitted to the test of Bible, tradition and reason, and in each case it has been found wanting. But although the historic episcopate is not essential to the church, in the sense that the church could not exist without it, there are solid reasons for retaining and extending the historic episcopate. Without it the church cannot achieve its full stature.

To speak thus of the fullness of the church is to use biblical categories. This is made clear by the chapter in this book which deals with the New Testament. The extended use of the phrase which is made here is further justified and con-

[1] Kirk, op. cit., p. 40.
[2] Br. George Every, S.S.M., *Theology*, March 1952, p. 83.

firmed by a study of *pleroma*[1] and its cognates in the New Testament.

It was God's good pleasure that in Christ at His advent all the fullness of the Godhead should dwell (Col. i. 19; ii. 9). The 'dispensation of the *fullness* of *times*' was to sum up all things in Christ.[2] Yet the second advent of the Lord was not to take place until 'the *times* of the Gentiles were *fulfilled*'.[3] The church which is the body of Christ is living 'between the times' of the Advent. Because it is the body of Christ, it is 'the *fullness* of him that filleth all in all'.[4] 'Of his *fullness* have we all received, and grace for grace'.[5]

The fullness of the church is further defined in the New Testament in terms which shew its full nature to be one, holy, catholic and apostolic. The catholic church is to contain the *fullness* of the Jews as well as the *fullness* of the Gentiles.[6] The church is to be holy, so that Paul can pray 'that ye may be strengthened with power through his Spirit in the inward man, that Christ may dwell in your hearts through faith to the end that ye being rooted and grounded in love may be strong to apprehend with all the saints . . . and to know the love of Christ which passeth knowledge, that ye may be *filled* with all the *fullness* of God'.[7] Other marks of the holiness which is to fill the members of the church are the Holy Spirit,[8] faith,[9] hope,[10] and joy.[11] Within the church there is to be full knowledge of God's will,[12] as well as the fruit of righteousness which comes from doing it.[13]

Great stress is laid in the New Testament on holiness as

---

[1] For the meanings of *pleroma*, cf. *Commentary on Ephesians*, J. A. Robinson (Macmillan, 1904), pp. 255–9. For the use of the term in gnostic systems, cf. *St. Paul and the Church of the Gentiles*, W. L. Knox (C.U.P., 1939), pp. 163–8; *Colossians and Philemon*, J. B. Lightfoot (Macmillan, 1890), pp. 262–71. Here we are concerned only with its exegesis in terms of biblical thought.

[2] Eph. 1: 10. cf. Gal. 4: 4.
[3] Luke 21: 24
[4] Eph. 1: 23.
[5] John 1: 16. cf. Col. 2: 10.
[6] Rom. 11: 12, 25.
[7] Eph. 3: 19. cf. Rom. 13: 10.
[8] Eph. 5: 18. cf. 1 Thess. 1: 5.
[9] Heb. 10: 22.
[10] Heb. 8: 11.
[11] John, 15: 11.
[12] Col. 1: 9; 4: 12.
[13] Phil. 1: 11.

part of the fullness of the church. But there is one important passage in which the apostolicity of the church is clearly connected with its unity and both with the fullness of Christ (Eph. iv. 10–13). In verse 10 it is made clear that by Christ's ascension into the heavens His material body has been removed so that through the church 'He may *fill* all things'. In the next verse, the apostolic ministry is distinguished from mere preaching of the apostolic gospel (evangelists) and from mere pastoral oversight (pastors). All church orders are given for 'the building up of the body of Christ': they do not constitute the church but they minister to it (verse 12). Through them we are to 'attain to the unity of the faith' and grow into 'the measure of the stature of the *fullness* of Christ' (verse 13).

These verses in Ephesians form perhaps the most definite exposition in the New Testament of the nature of the church's ministry. They provide the key to its understanding. It is common ground that the church must have a ministry just as the Kingdom could not come without the Messiah.[1] The historic episcopate embodies a special form of the ministry. It will be shewn that through it the apostolic ministry is continued and the unity of the faith built up. The historic episcopate is not constitutive of the church in the sense that without it the church would cease to exist. Rather, it is given to us, like the other elements of Christ's church, for the building up of His body, so that we may all attain to the measure of the stature of the fullness of Christ.

The 'apostolic succession' is the outward sign and instrument of the church's unity. Its primary meaning is the continuity of the apostolic church, which is 'sent' by Christ to the world. The apostolic ministry is derived from the apostolic church, as its organ and representative. In one sense the minister is the delegate of the church, who acts on behalf of his people in representing them before God. He is not, however, a mere delegate, registering the block-vote of his electors: he is a representative, chosen by God to execute

[1] cf. *The Ministry in the New Testament*, H. Riesenfeld in *The Root of the Vine* (Dacre, 1953), pp. 96–127.

his office over as well as on behalf of his people. He is the bearer of a commission from Christ to His church, although this ministry is always dependent upon the church, because his commission is received through it from Christ. The Church as a whole is a priestly body, and it is from the church that the priest derives his priesthood. The special commission that is given to the priest in no way diminishes the priesthood of the whole church: on the contrary, it heightens it.

To denote the historical continuity of this special commission, the phrase 'apostolic succession' can have two further meanings. It can symbolize a succession of bishops in a see (as the early fathers used it), or succession through episcopal consecration and ordination. It is the latter meaning which is used here.

The apostolic succession, in this sense, is the God-given focus of unity in the church. 'The episcopal office is a whole, one and indivisible, and the individual bishops share in it. In this collective episcopate, which is thus one, each bishop forms a living link not only between the Church of his own place, and the other local churches, but also between the church of to-day, and that of the generations that are past, and, we should add, of the generations that are still unborn.'[1] This link protects the 'deposit of the faith' and guards the wholeness of the apostolic message. 'As guardian of teaching, as an organ in the Body's continual life of grace—the Bishop sets forth the Gospel of God.'[2] The historic episcopate embodies the unity of the church vertically through time as well as horizontally through space. It does not guarantee unity[3] any more than it guarantees a splinterproof orthodoxy: but it is the God-given focus of unity. The return of those who have left this historically continuous unity is 'the return to a broken unity'.[4]

[1] A. G. Hebert, *The Apostolic Ministry*, p. 530. The writer is much indebted to this essay of Fr. Hebert, as well as to his criticisms of this chapter.

[2] A. M. Ramsey, *The Gospel and the Catholic Church* (Longmans, 1936), p. 83.

[3] Especially under the terms of the Anglican establishment. There have, it is true, been disastrous schisms from the Church of England, in which episcopacy has been regarded as one of the villains of the piece. But in the sixteenth century further splintering of the Church was inevitable in the whole Reformation situation, while in the eighteenth it was not episcopacy but its abuse which had such disastrous consequences.

[4] L. Newbigin, *The Reunion of the Church* (S.C.M. Press, 1948), p. 108.

In episcopal confirmation, the laity receive through the grace of the sacrament an outward pledge of their given unity in the apostolic church. At ordination the priest receives through the grace of orders the same pledge of unity. At the Holy Communion the people of God are all joined together in the sacrament of unity: the priest who celebrates becomes a special instrument of God's unifying activity. The consecration of bishops extends this same unity from the primitive church to the church of the future, from the local church to the church in distant lands. Thus the apostolic succession through the links of the historic succession embodies in the church the New Testament doctrine of its organic unity: it becomes the effectual symbol of this given unity. Without it, the church would not cease to exist. It is a mark of its fullness, since the church, when it attains its full stature, must shew forth its spiritual unity in the outward forms which God has given it.

The historic episcopate is also an effectual symbol of the relation of Christ to His church. There were three marks of the ministry of Our Lord. He was prophet, priest and king. These are also the marks of His church. The church is prophetic, for it is sent to preach the Gospel to the world; priestly, as St. Peter calls it, 'a spiritual house, a royal priesthood';[1] royal, for the royalty of the church consists in its acceptance of the royal humility of Christ and its consequent sharing in His ascension: 'if we suffer, we shall reign with Him'.[2]

The ministry of Christ, as we have seen, is continued not simply through the life of the whole church, but specially through the episcopal ministry, in which these same three marks are to be seen.[3] It is prophetic, because it is 'sent' to the church to proclaim Christ, just as Christ said to His disciples: 'As my Father hath sent me, even so send I you.'[4] It is priestly, because bishop and priest, by celebrating the Eucharist, are the human instruments whereby Christ represents on earth His eternal high priesthood. It is royal,

[1] 1 Peter, 2: 5.
[2] 2 Tim. 2: 12.
[3] cf. the biblical use of the same images both for the ministry of Christ and of His apostles (Riesenfeld, op. cit., pp. 106 ff.).
[4] John 20: 21.

for bishop and priest have special authority, exercised in humility after the example of Christ. Here the ministry is at once the bearer of authority to the church, and yet depends on the church for authority. After the same fashion, Christ is present within His body as its Head, yet the whole body is the body of Christ.

The church, then, is the embodiment of the Gospel, and the episcopal ministry is necessary for its fullness: bishop, priest and people working and worshipping together, not indeed with equal authority but taking no action without consulting together; in fact, like a family, the family of God. Thus the episcopal ministry is not only the God-given focus of unity, but follows the pattern of Christ. 'The presence at every stage of a principle prevails; for the impact of the Gospel moulds the church, and its order proclaims that the Christ is come in the flesh, and that his people are one family.'[1]

The status and functions of the episcopate and the priesthood, their grace and authority, are bestowed through the sacrament of orders. This is hardly surprising, for God's activity in the world, whether in creation or in redemption, in nature or in grace, is predominantly sacramental. The Incarnation is the supreme sacrament of all, uniquely expressive of God and uniquely instrumental of His purposes. The church, into which man is incorporated through Christ, has a sacramental nature, for through the church God both reveals Himself to men and reconciles men to Himself. Man's appropriation of God's redemption in Christ is continued through the sacraments as means of grace. The Christian sacraments are derived from Christ *through His church*.

The Church of England has distinguished the 'gospel sacraments' of Baptism and Eucharist because they are recorded in the Gospels as being instituted by Christ Himself.[2]

---

[1] Ramsey, op. cit., p. 80. cf. pp. 77–85 for a concise and brilliant treatment of this theme. But on p. 84 the author seems to have neglected his own warning: 'We are led, therefore, to affirm that the Episcopate is of the *esse* of the universal Church: but we must beware of mis-stating the issue.' What Dr. Ramsey has really shewn is that the Episcopate is *not* of the *esse* of the church, but belongs to the measure of the stature of the fullness of Christ.

[2] cf. Article XXV.

The 'lesser sacraments' do not pass unnoticed in the New Testament, but they cannot be said to be instituted by Christ, according to the Gospels, in the same way as the two great sacraments. Even if modern critical scholarship could claim to disprove the historical foundation of the accounts of their institution in the words of Jesus, the Anglican distinction still holds good. For they both remain embedded in the inspired writings of the New Testament and faithfully reflect the priorities of the Apostolic church. To make the Eucharist depend for its *validity* on the episcopal ordination of the celebrant is to magnify a 'lesser sacrament' so that it becomes more important than a 'gospel sacrament'. This is unapostolic, unanglican, and unreasonable.

What, then, is the point of the Anglican insistence on the historic episcopate and episcopal ordination? The sacrament of orders is 'a sure witness and effectual sign of grace'. *It is a real means of grace*, whereby the candidate for Holy Orders is commissioned by God for his special exercise of the apostolate within the church: this takes place as in prayer the bishop, and the priests around him, lay their hands upon him amid the prayers of the congregation. From the earliest days of episcopacy the administration of this sacrament was put into the hands of the bishop, because he is the representative of the apostolic church, the effectual symbol of its unity and commissioned for this special exercise of the apostolic ministry. For the same reason an episcopally ordained minister adminsters the initiatory sacrament of baptism wherever possible, and celebrates the Eucharist: these are two of the apostolic tasks to which he has been called by God and set apart by the church to perform.

The Church of England requires episcopal consecration and ordination for reasons similar to those for episcopal confirmation. These two sacraments are in some ways similar. The practice of the laying on of hands in the early church, from which confirmation is probably derived,[1] does not seem to have been uniformly carried out. According to the New Testament, baptism, not confirmation, is the sacrament

[1] Even this is not certain. 'The link is admittedly fragile.' G. W. H. Lampe, *The Seal of the Spirit* (Longmans, 1951), p. 322.

of initiation into Christ, and because it involves a sharing of Christ's baptism, it imparts the gift of the Holy Spirit. The sacrament of confirmation, however, is grounded in the New Testament and preserves important elements of apostolic doctrine and practice. It is not *essential* for membership of the church, but it is a real means of grace which must be gladly retained for full membership. Episcopal consecration and ordination are rightly required for similar reasons. The confirmand has been said to receive 'perhaps his ordination to an apostolate' in the sense of a commission for service in the church's mission. This is effectually symbolized by his reception of the ancient sign of blessing and of 'solidarity' with the bishop as the representative of the apostolic church.[1] The similarity of episcopal consecration and ordination is now clear. These sacraments are required not because the church would cease to exist without them, but that it may realize its true nature and shew forth the stature of the fullness of Christ.

All sacraments are dependent on the church and not the church upon the sacraments. Sacraments are derived from Christ through the church, and it is through the church that they are administered. But the church is divided. How can any part of the church make an effective offering on behalf of the whole body of the church in those very sacraments concerning which it is divided from other parts of the body?

As far as the ordering of His church is concerned, Christ gives to a priest through the grace of orders both spiritual power and spiritual authority in His church. (The two are formally distinct, although ultimately inseparable.) Both are received through the church. 'Capacity to exercise authority, and *a fortiori* capacity to transmit it, reside in the office held rather than in the person of who holds it. And without disputing the sense in which a bishop can never cease to be a bishop, we may surely maintain that his capacity to transmit his authority to others is dependent upon the condition that his status as the holder of some definite episcopal office is still recognized by the body itself.'[2]

[1] cf. Lampe, op. cit., ibid.
[2] O. C. Quick, *The Christian Sacraments* (Nisbet, 1927), p. 143. cf. pp. 123–54 for an elaboration of the theme.

Both the spiritual power and authority are defective because the body is divided.[1] In the re-united church, the grace of orders will bestow upon the priest the fullness of spiritual power belonging to his office. Because of the divisions of the church,[2] his authorization is now still partial and incomplete. This applies both to episcopal and non-episcopal orders. The authority of the ministry is constricted, as though by a tourniquet, within parts of the body. God uses these different ministries in different parts of the body.

All orders, then, are defective: but they are not all equally defective. The church officer of the Seventh Day Adventists, the Presbyterian minister and the Anglican priest are not all 'on the same level'. In the first place, those ordained into the apostolic succession are given a spiritual grace and authorization from the Risen Christ through the church which itself goes back in historical continuity to the Apostles of the primitive church and so to the historical Jesus Himself. They are ordained into the form of ministry which gives full stature to the church. Even so, their authorization is incomplete, but it is less defective than that of the non-episcopally ordained minister. Secondly, not all ministers are ordained to the same functions. Only the priest, for instance, is authorized to exercise the ministry of absolution. Thirdly, a right intention is necessary for the right appropriation of sacraments. So far as Holy Orders are concerned, this means an intention on the part of those concerned with the sacrament 'to do as the church does', and an orthodox confession on the part of the ordinand. Non-episcopal ordinations may leave room here for legitimate doubt.

[1] It has been objected that this implies that Christ's authority was deficient, since the Jews rejected Him. This objection is superficial. Christ's authority was given to Him by His Father and did not depend upon men (John v: 43; viii: 42). But ministerial authority is not given to a man straight from Heaven: it is bestowed by the Risen Christ through His divided church.

[2] Here the 'church' means 'Christ's church militant here in earth'. It has been objected (E. L. Mascall, *Corpus Christi*, Longmans 1953, p. 22) that the theory of defective orders leaves out of account the church expectant and triumphant. This does not follow. It is of course true that the church in heaven and earth forms a unity, but this unity is not simple and mathematical. Christ has committed the ordering of the church militant to the members of His body here on earth. We are related *eschatologically* to the greater church. The further suggestion that our bishops will still be bishops in heaven (Mascall, op. cit., p. 30) is purely speculative and does not affect the theory of defective orders.

The fact that all orders are defective does not mean that sacraments thereby cease to be real 'pledges of assurance'. Wherever there is a real intention to carry out both the form and the matter of the sacraments, God uses them in accordance with His promise. Sacraments are sure because God is faithful. Defective orders do not diminish the grace of the sacrament any more than does the unworthiness of the priest.[1] Nor does the admission that all orders are to some degree defective diminish the reasonable claims of episcopacy. The historic episcopate belongs to the *plene esse* of the church.

It should now become apparent that the word 'valid' can be a confusing term in ecumenical discussion, when it is contrasted with 'efficacious'. Often it is used loosely as a confusing synonym for 'episcopally ordained'. But its proper meaning is ambiguous. If it means 'guaranteed', then it implies that 'valid' orders guarantee the church, whereas in fact orders are dependent upon the church. Anglicans should beware of throwing around words like 'valid' and 'invalid' for Anglican orders have themselves been called in question.[2] Those who live in glass houses should not throw stones! For the fact that the church is disastrously divided is sufficient in itself to prevent any orders being 'guaranteed'. But the real objection to guarantees lies at a far deeper level than this. The craving for guarantees arises from an over-burdened sense of spiritual fear and spiritual insecurity; the church lives not by guarantee but by grace.

On the other hand, if 'valid' is used to mean 'legitimate' (and 'invalid' to mean 'illegitimate'), this implies that the church stands not under grace but under law; that when men found it unavoidable to initiate fresh orders in order to reform part of the church into a spiritual body, God *ought* not to have used those very ministries which it is admitted that He *has* used. 'Non-episcopal ministries are ministries *de facto* no doubt, but not necessarily *de jure*'.[3] What does *de jure*

---

[1] cf. Article XXVI, 'Of the unworthiness of the Ministers, which hinders not the effect of the sacrament.'

[2] cf. Pope Leo XIII's *Apostolicae Curae*: 'We pronounce and declare that ordinations carried out according to the Anglican rite have been and are absolutely null and utterly void.' (*Anglican Orders*, S.P.C.K., 1932, p. 14.)

[3] Kirk, op. cit., p. 44.

mean? *De jure episcoporum?* This is mere tautology: of course non-episcopal ministries are not constituted according to episcopal requirements. *De jure divino?* God may break the church's canon law, but He cannot disregard His own decree. He cannot do in practice what He has refused in principle.

It is more natural to speak about degrees of plenitude than of validity, more natural to think of orders as more or less defective rather than more or less invalid. In this essay therefore the phrase 'defective orders' has been used instead of 'invalid orders'. (Ordinations by an *episcopus vagans* are not invalid but null and void, because they are not acts of the church.) In our view, most of the various ministries are efficacious, but all in different ways and for varying functions. All are in varying degrees defective—and that is one pressing reason for re-union.

The goal of re-union is Christendom re-united under the historic episcopate, not merely because this is the only practical goal for re-union,[1] but also because the historic episcopate belongs to the full stature of the church. Although it is not *essential* to the life of the church, it offers the focus of unity, the guardianship of the Word and Sacraments, of the faith and the flock of Christ: it presents the form of the church stamped by the impress of Christ and His Gospel. In this essay an attempt has been made to describe the function of the historic episcopate and to explain its meaning. *The function of the historic episcopate must conform to this apostolic pattern.* It would be ludicrous to insist on something to which neither meaning could be given nor function attached.

In some quarters, however, there is a craze not for description but for definition. That is quite a different matter. The Church of England, in her wisdom, has never made any authoritative definition of the historic episcopate. Such a

[1] Contrast with this view the statement in *The Doctrine of the Church and Christian Re-union*, A. C. Headlam (Murray, 1910), p. 269. 'It is not then because I believe the Historic Episcopate is necessary for valid Orders, but *because I believe it is necessary to secure Christian unity*, that I believe that it must be the rule of a re-united Church.' (Italics mine.)

definition would not only ill accord with the whole Anglican method and ethos. It would not even be possible to make.

The historic episcopate is a form of God's sacramental activity. The fullness of its meaning can only be known from experience. As such, it can and must be described: it cannot be defined. Definition is a 'statement of the precise meaning of a term'; description is a 'representation in words enabling the hearer or reader to form an idea of an object or sensation or incident or like'. Ultimates cannot be defined. It is possible, for instance, to describe 'the right' and 'the good'. But the fact that there is no agreement about their definition— and some moral philosophers consider them to be indefinable —does not detract in the least from the reality of moral obligation and value. In a similar way, sacraments cannot be defined. No one thinks it necessary to state precisely what happens at baptism before Holy Baptism may be administered. No one is excommunicated because he cannot state the exact mode of Christ's presence at the Eucharist. Sacraments are given by God to be 'done' and not to gratify an itch for theological definition. No one can be expected to define the indefinable. The episcopate is a sacred office, a 'mysterion'. Where there are ultimate mysteries, the Church of England marks buoys at the two extremes of that broad channel through which a passage may safely be made. These buoys must be precisely marked, and the passage itself clearly described and its limits defined. That task has been attempted in this essay.

The Church of England, although she has not 'defined' the historic episcopate, has gladly accepted it. She has studiously avoided 'unchurching' those churches which have not yet got episcopal orders. These other churches have great gifts to contribute to the coming great church of all Christendom. But it is not true that 'all have won and all shall have prizes'. Rather all will bring prizes but no one will have won. Then and only then will the church display the fullness of her life. Because the Church of England is both catholic and reformed, her contributions will be many; and these will include the historic episcopate which is capable of giving full expression of Christ's Gospel in the ordering of His church.

It is no merit of our Church that she has such rich treasures to bring. The pages of church history often make unedifying reading, and the Anglican record is no better than others. But the Most High rules in the kingdom of men, and He turns even the wrath of men to His praise.

VII

THE NEXT STEP

K. M. Carey

So far in this book we have tried to examine the problem of
the historic episcopate from a theological and, to some extent,
from an historical point of view. The writers of the previous
chapters have each attempted to assess the religious value of
episcopacy and by opening windows on different periods of
the Church's life, to see how the Church in general, and the
Church of England in particular has regarded episcopacy
and where she has placed it in her scheme of religious
priorities.

The first chapter has placed our theme within its proper
biblical perspective of the kingdom, the church and the
ministry. The New Testament chapter has cleared the ground
of undue emphasis on the niceties of biblical terminology over
ministerial offices. From an examination of Spirit and structure in the New Testament period the vital principle
emerges that the structure of the ministry is not the medium
but the expression of the Spirit. The next chapter demon-
strates that while the Fathers cannot give us answers to
questions which are different from theirs, we can profit not
from their conclusions but from their underlying attitudes.
The essay on the early Anglican fathers shews that amid all
the confusions, conflicts and extremes of the Anglican reformation, there emerged a solid body of Anglican opinion
which saw the theological importance of the historic episcopate without 'unchurching' those churches which did not
possess it. The third historical chapter deals with the nineteenth century and here the theological issues are put in their
true perspective: the main emphasis was on the rediscovery
of a 'high' doctrine of the church, which was often buttressed
by a rigid doctrine of the ministry, although the latter was

really peripheral to the former. The penultimate chapter attempts to make a systematic presentation of the theology of the episcopate as of the *plene esse* of the church, and subjects it to the traditional sources of Anglican authority.

We are thus convinced that our Church has in fact, and rightly, placed a very high value on episcopacy and we believe that even if episcopacy cannot be regarded as of the *esse* of the church's existence, it belongs to its *plene esse* and therefore to the *esse* of the church's final unity.

In 1955 the Convocations of Canterbury and York must decide what their relationship with the Church of South India shall be. Three solutions are possible: (1) a decision to maintain the present position, (2) a decision to recognize the Bishops and Presbyters of the C.S.I. ordained after inauguration as true Bishops and Presbyters, (3) a decision to recognize the C.S.I. as part of the true Catholic Church and therefore to enter into full communion with her. We make no secret of the fact that in writing this book we hope and pray for the last solution. We believe that in full communion with the C.S.I. the Church of England can gain much and give much and lose nothing that is essential. For if the previous chapters have convinced the reader that episcopacy is neither of the *esse*, still less of the *bene esse*, but definitely and inescapably of the *plene esse* of the Church, then in the Church of South India we are confronted by a Church which believes as we do and with which there can be no bar to communion. We are encouraged that this conclusion should be so strikingly endorsed by the recent Report on South India published in 1953 by the Metropolitan's Committee of the Mar Thoma Church.

It is, however, only honest that we should admit that any step forward is bound to involve the Church of England in certain anomalies. Wherever in God's world sin exists there are bound to be anomalous situations. What matters is not that we should be paralyzed by the situation so that we are unable to move, nor that we should pretend that there can be any logical solution to a problem whose roots lie far back in a sinful and illogical past, but that we should realize that God has already made us one and that our vocation is to express that unity by obedience to what God is saying now. In the life of the Church the greatest anomaly of all is division: we must beware lest we strain at a few gnats and swallow a camel. Nor in recognizing the danger of a too logical approach to the problem need we fear that we are breaking away from the temper and tone of the Church in past ages and especially from the historic position of Anglicanism. Previous chapters of this book have shown that the Church has in the past been ready on occasions to overlook anomalies which were small in comparison with the scandal of disunity. The Nicene Fathers were willing to overlook grave irregularities in the past method of consecrating bishops in the Egyptian Church provided that unity was secured for the future. Nor need we feel any sense of shame that when bishops were restored to the Scottish Church in the seventeenth century they accepted the existing presbyterian ministers and did not insist on their re-ordination.[1]

But if here and elsewhere in this book we have quoted instances of where the Church has been enabled to transcend anomalies for the sake of unity we have no wish to use these instances as precedents. For we are faced now by an entirely unprecedented situation. Never before in the history of Christendom has a group of Churches episcopal and non-episcopal come together into union *on an episcopal basis*. It is this fact which makes the Church of South India unique and uniquely challenging. As the second Synod of the Church of South India said in 1950: 'We are united in one Church; our parent Churches are divided. If it is now insisted that we state what our permanent relation with them is to be, we can only say that we can be content with nothing except that they should be united as we are. So long as they remain divided our position must remain anomalous from the point of view of any one of the divided Churches. But from the point of view of the historic faith of the Church we must surely judge that the real anomaly, the real scandal, is that the Church should be divided. We have promised at the end of thirty years to give equal weight to two principles; that our own ministry shall be one and that we shall maintain

[1] See G. B. Henderson, *The Claims of the Church of Scotland*, pp. 85 and 91.

and extend full communion with our parent Churches. As things stand, these two principles are irreconcilable. They can only be reconciled when the parent Churches now divided are united. Our act of union is an act of faith in the Holy Spirit that He will bring this about. We cannot therefore say more than the Constitution has said about what our successors will do in circumstances which we pray may be profoundly different from those in which we now are.'

'Our act of union is an act of faith in the Holy Spirit . . .' It cannot be said too strongly that in the Church of South India we are dealing with a Church which has taken, and is taking, seriously Our Lord's promise that the Holy Spirit would lead the Church into all truth. It is to the shame of the parent Churches that too often in their discussions about unity they seem only concerned with what the Spirit has done in the past and hardly at all with what He wills to do in the future.

There are, however, several questions about the Church of South India to which many loyal Anglicans would wish to have an answer before they could commit themselves whole-heartedly to any scheme of full communion.

1. *There are, and there may continue to be even after the thirty years period, a number of non-episcopally ordained presbyters in the Church of South India.*

No one who holds episcopacy in its full historic sense to be of the *plene esse* of the Church would deny that this is an anomaly. But it may well be questioned whether it is of such importance as to constitute a barrier or even the cause of delay to full communion. In the first place it is clear in the minds of those who are responsible for the government of the C.S.I. that God has used this anomaly: all the uniting Churches would testify that already they have learnt much from what each of them has brought into the common fund of wisdom and experience. They started by recognizing each other's ministries and their experience since union has fortified them in this act of faith. Secondly, as is well-known, it is the rule that all ordinands in the Church are for the future to be episcopally ordained. Thirdly, it is a fact that the majority of men going out from non-episcopal Churches to serve in the C.S.I.

are waiting for ordination (which will then of course be episcopal) until they arrive in South India. Fourthly—and from a theological point of view this is perhaps the most important argument—it is the intention of the C.S.I. to be and to remain an episcopal Church. Bishop W. E. Collins, the High Church Bishop of Gibraltar, wrote: 'The whole point of corporate life is that one weak spot does not, and many weak spots do not, destroy the body. A truer image would be that of a coat of mail, in which one broken link does not destroy the continuity of the rest, or a rope, which is continuous even though no single fibre subsists for more than a foot or two of its length. Of course the truest image of all is a living body, in which the life of the whole actually repairs and makes good the need of the part. A mechanical theory which forgets the solidarity of the body is hopelessly wrong. . . . *I* should not hesitate to say that the very meaning of the corporate life of the Church is that it guarantees to us the continuity of the Ministry, and makes good accidental defects, where the intention of the Church has been maintained as regards its Ministry, and where its practical action has been continuous. The idea is not familiar to us, but it is quite in accordance with primitive use, and quite familiar in Eastern theology, that *that* is Holy Order which the Church recognizes as such, and that the Church of its inherent life makes good any defects which there may be in that which it recognizes.'[1]

2. *The Sacrament of Confirmation is not at present universally administered in the C.S.I.*

It is true that episcopal confirmation is not universally required as a pre-requisite of Holy Communion. But we should be highly selective and unwise if we were to regard modern Anglican practice as the norm. There is plenty of evidence to show that, before the Reformation, Confirmation was often more honoured in the breach than in the observance and there are periods in our history since the Reformation when Confirmation has been widely neglected or administered in such a way as would cast doubt on its validity

[1] See *Life of W. E. Collins*, by A. J. Mason, pp. 164-5.

judged by modern practice. Moreover there is evidence that the Roman Church in the eighteenth century sent out to Travancore Vicars-Apostolic with power to confirm as there were no bishops on the spot to administer the sacrament. We need not, however, go back into history to find examples of presbyteral confirmation in the Church of Rome. In the new decree on Confirmation (issued in the official Papal organ, *Acta Apostolicae Sedis* in Sept./Oct. 1946, to come into force on 1 January, 1947),[1] the principle is clearly conceded although the principles of administration are carefully guarded.

But the overwhelming argument is not negative but positive: it is the argument of pastoral necessity. In South India as in Mediaeval England it is almost impossible for bishops to get round their dioceses sufficiently often to confirm all those who are ready and desirous of receiving the Holy Communion. Confirmation, therefore, or its equivalent, is still, and for some time is likely to be, administered in some dioceses by presbyters. It is surely not without significance that in the Diocese of Madura and Ramnad the official figures for 1948 (the first full year of the dioceses' existence) show that in the C.M.S. area the proportion of confirmed to baptized adults was 49 per cent; in the S.P.G. area the proportion was 62 per cent; while in the ex-Congregational area the proportion of those admitted to full communion (i.e. by some form of presbyteral confirmation) was 72 per cent. The Bishop of the diocese, who recognizes and welcomes the fact that the practice of episcopal confirmation is increasing, nevertheless points to these figures as showing 'a very important element of strength in presbyteral confirmation.'

3. The historic Creeds are not obligatory in public worship and members of the C.S.I. are not bound to accept any particular interpretation of the various clauses.

There are two misunderstandings here which can quite easily be cleared up. First, when the C.S.I. refused to make the recital of the Creed obligatory at every service there was

[1] I owe this reference to Bishop Lesslie Newbigin.

133

no intention of countenancing any diminution of belief in the historic faith of Christendom. It was rather to make provision for services where the recital of the Creed was considered to be unnecessary, as for example when in the Church of England the Creed is often omitted in celebrations of the Holy Communion or in non-liturgical services. In the Liturgy of the C.S.I., which is increasingly being used and which is regarded by liturgical experts as a model, the Nicene Creed is ordered to be said or sung after the Gospel. Secondly, when in the note on assent to the Creed the C.S.I. 'does not intend to demand the assent of individuals to every word and phrase in them or to exclude reasonable interpretation . . .' the intention is not to include among the worshippers those whose faith in the cardinal doctrines of the Church is inadequate but to recognize honestly a state of affairs which exists in every Church. It would ill become the Church of England to cavil at such honesty seeing that Churchmen of of every school of thought have always allowed themselves 'reasonable' interpretation of such phrases as 'descended into hell' or 'sitteth on the right hand of God'. And English Churchmen of even the straitest sect are not prepared to leave the Church of England because there is general consent in the Church to the view expressed in 'Doctrine in the Church of England' that 'Assent to formularies and the use of liturgical language in public worship should be understood as signifying such general acceptance without implying detailed assent to every phrase or proposition thus employed.'

It would be neither generous nor honest for the Church of England to demand or expect of the C.S.I. a standard of practice or belief stricter than she is herself able to maintain.

4. *Union with the C.S.I. will split the Church of England.*

This is perhaps the most difficult argument of all for it rests both on an appeal to the emotions and on an assumption which cannot possibly be verified. In the first place it is easy to scare those who by temperament and tradition are inclined to play for safety. Any who have gloried in the comprehensiveness of the Church of England must necessarily view with trepidation any step which may reduce the bounds of that comprehension. To many—and probably to the vast majority of English Churchmen—it is the chief glory of the Church of England that men of widely different theological and ecclesiastical presuppositions can be held together in one Church using one Prayer Book and governed by one ministry. But there are limits to comprehensiveness: for example, the Church of England at the moment can comprehend those who hold the theory that episcopacy is of the *esse* of the Church and those who hold that it is only of the *bene esse*. So long as neither side insists on pressing its theory until it becomes a matter of absolute principle, that comprehensiveness can continue to exist. But the moment one side or the other demands that the Church should define its theory of episcopacy and exalt it into a dogma, comprehensiveness breaks down. Either side has the right to advocate its theory by all legitimate means but in no foreseeable future is the Church of England as a whole likely to embrace as a matter of faith either theory. Indeed, it has been one of the main purposes of this book to show that neither theory is theologically sufficient to fit the facts.

Secondly, the argument that union with the C.S.I. will split the Church of England is merely an assumption. Not to put too fine a point upon it, it is the sort of unconscious bluff which is sometimes employed by those who wish to end a discussion without having fairly examined the evidence. In this book we have urged again and again that the Church of England has much to gain *and no point of principle to lose* in going into full Communion with the C.S.I. We believe that to be true. And we believe further that the Church of England must decide on what are the essential and indispensable doctrines of the Faith before she can become again the Church of the English people. The last fifty years have seen a strong attempt to force on the Church of England an interpretation of its formularies—particularly as they relate to the doctrine of the ministry—which neither theology nor the history of our Church can substantiate. A split may come from within the Church if this attempt is continued. But we believe that such a split, whether it comes from within or without, is neither necessary nor expedient. If it does come it will be because the Church of England has been forced to depart from her historic refusal to define what is indefinable.

5. *There is no need to hurry: let us see what will happen at the end of the thirty years' period.*

This is the last and the most dangerous of the arguments which are brought against a decisive step being taken in 1955. It is dangerous because it may appear to be the answer of true statesmanship, and it may for that reason deceive even those who are convinced that on other grounds there is no bar to immediate union. Quite possibly if the Convocations waited for only ten years there would be much less difficulty in reaching practical unanimity, for there is no doubt that the tide of opinion is beginning to flow strongly in favour of the South India Church. Many of those who have been out to see for themselves have returned from India profoundly impressed by the new Church;[1] others have realized that the picture that they had formed in England was widely distorted; and there is no lack of evidence that in the Church of South India itself there is a rapidly growing conviction that episcopacy has brought them more than they had hoped or foreseen.

But to delay for even ten years is both dangerous and unrealistic. It is dangerous because it is always dangerous to postpone a decision which Truth is pressing on the conscience. If there is no other reason to delay then it is clearly wrong to delay simply in the hope of becoming more sure. It is unrealistic because it is a refusal to face the facts of the world situation. The world, in which the Church is set to minister, is not static: it is on the move. In Asia it is moving very fast indeed. The Church in South India is not only confronted by vast masses of non-Christians to whom our Western divisions are quite unintelligible: it also has to combat the growing forces of nationalism and Communism. No one can predict how

[1] For example, Fr. Dalby, Superior General of S.S.J.E., who returned in 1953 from a visit to India, is reported in the News Sheet of the British C.S.I. Council (Nov. 1953) to have said: 'One thing I give C.S.I. absolutely full marks for every time is that they really do show what Episcopacy is. Their bishops are leaders and centres of unity and peace for Christian bodies of different traditions.'

those forces will spread in India. It may be that within a few years the Church may be driven underground by Communism or stripped of its European leadership by nationalism. If this should happen it is of the utmost importance that the Christian witness should be united and strong. If the Church in South India should be cut off from the Church in England it would nevertheless be strengthened immeasurably by knowing that it was in full communion with its parent bodies. The urgency can only be realized by those who know the compulsion of the situation in which the Church is set, and the burden of the Gospel. Those who are in that position have no doubt about the contribution that the Church of England could make. If, then, we in this country adopt the policy of 'wait and see' we may well find that the help which we shall eventually give will be too little and too late.

The question is urgent for another reason: the formation of the World Council of Churches was a great step forward in ecumenical relations, but already there are many who see great dangers in the growing habit of inter-Church discussions. As we 'stay together' in the World Council we may become so accustomed to the policy of issuing statements that we lose the ideal of moving forward into unity. And federalism is no substitute for the full organic unity which alone can be the answer to the prayer of Christ that 'all may be one'. There are indeed many problems of faith and order which must be faced before all the member Churches of the World Council can become organically one. But in the Church of South India we are confronted by a Church which already has all the marks of true Catholicity and which is already moving forward into the fullness of Catholic practice.

Finally, it is possible that in making this plea for full organic union with the Church of South India at the earliest possible date we shall be accused of appealing to the hearts of our fellow Churchmen rather than to their heads. To this we can only answer that we have tried to see the problems as honestly as we could and that we believe the distinction between heart and head to be utterly unreal. For truth is in Jesus Christ and in the fact of His Atonement. He has broken down the middle wall of partition: He has made us one: and our understanding of that stupendous fact will be conditioned as much by our obedience as by our logic. In a sermon on the Revelation through Love, Bishop B. F. Westcott said: 'Not on the first Easter Morning only have believers been inclined to claim absolute permanence for their own partial apprehension of Truth: not on the first Easter Morning only, but in this later age I will venture to say more than then. . . . It is impossible not to fear, when in the widespread searching of hearts men cling almost desperately to traditional phrases and customs, that we may forget the call of Christ to occupy new regions of thought and labour in His Name.'

INDEX OF AUTHORITIES CITED